MANAGING CYBERSECURITY RESOURCES

MANAGING CYBERSECURITY RESOURCES

A Cost-Benefit Analysis

Lawrence A. Gordon
and
Martin P. Loeb

McGraw-Hill

New York   Chicago   San Francisco   Lisbon   London   Madrid   Mexico City
Milan   New Delhi   San Juan   Seoul   Singapore   Sydney   Toronto

The *McGraw·Hill* Companies

1 2 3 4 5 6 7 8 9 0 DOC/DOC 0 9 8 7 6 5

ISBN 0-07-145285-0

This publication is designed to provide accurate and authoritative information in regard to the subject matter covered. It is sold with the understanding that the publisher is not engaged in rendering legal, accounting, or other professional service. If legal advice or other expert assistance is required, the services of a competent professional person should be sought.
> —*From a declaration of principles jointly adopted by a committee of the American Bar Association and a committee of publishers.*

McGraw-Hill books are available at special quantity discounts to use as premiums and sales promotions, or for use in corporate training programs. For more information, please write to the Director of Special Sales, McGraw-Hill Professional, Two Penn Plaza, New York, NY 10121-2298. Or contact your local bookstore.

 This book is printed on recycled, acid-free paper containing a minimum of 50% recycled, de-inked fiber.

Library of Congress Cataloging-in-Publication Data

Gordon, Lawrence A.
    Managing cybersecurity resources : a cost-benefit analysis / by Lawrence A. Gordon and Martin P. Loeb.
    p.   cm.
    Includes bibliographical references and index.
    ISBN 0-07-145285-0 (hardcover : alk. paper)   1. Business—Data
    processing—Security measures.   2. Computer security.   3. Information
    technology—Security measures.   4. Data protection.   I. Loeb, Martin, P.   II. Title.
    HF5548.37.G67   2005
    658.4'78—dc22
                                                                    2005014300

Contents

v

PREFACE

HOW CAN MANAGERS determine the optimal level of funding for information and computer system security? How should these funds be allocated among competing cybersecurity projects? How can chief information security officers (CISOs) develop an effective business case for cybersecurity projects? These questions, which are central to this book, were among the first questions we addressed at the beginning of the millennium when we began our research on the economic aspects of cybersecurity. More to the point, the primary objective of this book is to present a framework to assist organizations in determining the appropriate amount to spend on cybersecurity activities and to efficiently allocate such resources. This framework is based on the principle of cost-benefit analysis. To our knowledge, this is the first book to provide such a framework.

As business school professors with backgrounds in managerial economics and decision support information systems, we have always had a keen professional interest in the value and use of information for managerial decision making. However, over the last decade, it has become clear to us that the rapid growth of information technology (IT) in general, and specifically the Internet, demands that our teaching and research agendas be transformed to reflect the realities of the digital economy. Chief among these realities is the growing importance of cybersecurity.

There is a rapidly emerging general realization by those working in information technology, as well as senior management (e.g., chief executive officers and chief financial officers), that the economic aspects of information security must be placed on an equal footing with the technical aspects of protecting computer networks. However, there is much confusion with respect to economic and financial concepts as applied to cybersecurity resource management. For example, the numerous articles on rates of return on information security investments appearing in a variety of professional magazines are frequently contradictory and error-prone—seemingly oblivious to the long-standing literature in accounting, economics, and finance.

This book is intended to provide a sound guide for managers dealing with the economic and financial aspects of information security. As such, this book should be a valuable resource for information security managers, financial managers responsible for the allocation of cybersecurity dollars, and other IT personnel involved in the budgeting aspects of organizational resources associated with information security. This book is also intended for use in university courses, both at the graduate and at the advanced undergraduate levels, covering the economic and financial aspects of information security.

This book does not assume any previous background in economics or information security on the part of the reader. However, some material in Chapters 2 and 4 requires a moderate degree of mathematical sophistication. Readers can skim the mathematics in these chapters and still understand the main message.

The plan of the book is as follows. In the first chapter, we discuss the importance of cybersecurity and consider some of the key issues that affect the process of managing cybersecurity resources. The second chapter provides an economic framework for managing cybersecurity resources. This framework is based on the principle of cost-benefit analysis. The third chapter discusses cost concepts and empirical evidence related to assessing the actual costs and benefits of cybersecurity breaches. Determining the right amount to spend on cybersecurity is the subject of the fourth chapter. The fifth chapter discusses the role that risk plays in the allocation of cybersecurity resources. Chapter 6 provides a generic business case approach for securing the funding deemed necessary. Cybersecurity auditing is the subject of the seventh chapter. Chapter 8 examines the role of cybersecurity in national security, and the final chapter provides some concluding comments related to important cybersecurity issues.

ACKNOWLEDGMENTS

WE WISH TO EXPRESS our sincere appreciation to the many people who have helped us in forming many of the views expressed in this book. These people include, but are not limited to, Michael Ball, Nancy Blanco, Lawrence Bodin, Kate Campbell, Marianne Emerson, Howard Frank, Gary Hayward, Joseph JaJa, William Lucyshyn, Cara Ramsey, Robert Richardson, William Semancik, Tashfeen Sohail, Chih-Yang Tseng, and Lei Zhou. Their help has come through discussions of various research projects, through discussions concerning the application of some of the concepts presented in the book to problems confronting specific organizations, and/or through comments on earlier drafts of this book. Discussions with numerous unnamed participants at various forums, workshops, conferences, and seminars, where many of the ideas expressed in this book were initially presented, also contributed to the writing of this book.

Finally, we wish to thank our wives (Hedy and Carol) for their moral support of the work related to this book. Their continued support provides a source of strength for all of our endeavors in life.

INTRODUCTION

Let's face it; when you cease to dream, you cease to live.

—ROBERT H. SMITH (BUSINESSMAN AND PHILANTHROPIST)[1]

RE YOU WORRIED about the security of the information stored in your home and office computers? Are you worried about the security of the organizations that hold your personal, financial, and medical information? If not, you should be worried—or at least concerned.

Every day, individuals and organizations become victims of information security breaches that have significant financial implications. Indeed, the Internet revolution continues to generate new opportunities for savvy criminals to infiltrate computer systems.

---

[1] Taken from a speech delivered by Robert H. Smith on February 3, 2005, at a ceremony announcing his $30 million gift to the University of Maryland.

These infiltrations are what we refer to as breaches in cybersecurity. To gain peace of mind and prevent future breaches, most individuals and organizations take steps to implement some level of cybersecurity. However, given the unpredictable nature of these breaches, cybersecurity decisions are often based on gut instinct rather than on sound economic analysis. In order to rectify this situation, this book presents guidelines for efficiently managing cybersecurity resources within organizations.[2] These guidelines are based on the economic principle of cost-benefit analysis.[3]

The Internet revolution

The *Internet* is an electronic communications network that connects computers around the world and is truly the result of some big-time dreaming by several creative people. Like most great inventions, the Internet (as we know it today) evolved over time. This evolution is described by the Internet Society (2003).

In the last decade, we witnessed an unprecedented information and technological explosion led by the Internet revolution. This interconnectivity changed the way people work and play, and, in essence, the way they think about life. People now use the Internet to keep in touch with family and friends, shop online, research legal and medical questions, and entertain themselves. The Inter-

---

[2] Cybersecurity resources include human resources. Thus, the allocation of security resources includes the allocation of resources for the hiring and training of employees to strengthen the organization's information security. While such resource allocation falls within the scope of this book, the book does not deal with how best to manage the employees who are actively engaged in information security activities. Moreover, while the focus of this book is on managing cybersecurity resources within organizations, nearly all of the discussions could also apply to managing cybersecurity resources for individuals.

[3] Anderson (2001) argues that one needs to view information security problems from an economics perspective. This theme is also developed in Gordon and Loeb (2001b).

net also changed the way organizations operate. For example, the Internet allows employees to work from practically any location. In addition, it allows organizations to make direct purchases from vendors and to sell to customers from around the world in real time (i.e., instantaneously).

For an organization or an individual, the benefits and costs of using the Internet are largely associated with *network externalities,* or spillovers to a user of the network resulting from the fact that many others are using the same network. Benefits from network externalities are the positive spillovers to a user of the network resulting from the fact that many others are also using the same network. For example, the fact that you can connect your individual computer to the same network used by your banks, your employer, and your friends greatly increases the value of being connected to this network. The phenomenal rate of growth of the Internet in the late 1990s was largely due to such positive network externalities—as more individuals and organizations connected to the Internet, it became more attractive for others to also get connected.

While the benefits of the Internet are numerous, the Internet also creates some significant costs. One such cost, which has already wreaked havoc on countless individuals and organizations, is related to cybersecurity breaches. Computer *viruses* (malicious computer programs that cause malfunctions in a computer system), identity theft, and corporate espionage are among the best-known cybersecurity breaches. Viruses like "MyDoom" and "Code Red" can shut down thousands of computers in a matter of minutes. The costs associated with such viruses have been estimated to be in the billions of U.S. dollars, when aggregated across all of the organizations and individuals affected by these viruses.

The daily newspapers frequently include stories of cybersecurity breaches that have potentially devastating effects on organizations and individuals. For example, on March 15, 2005, the *Wall Street Journal* ran a thought-provoking story concerning identity theft affecting hundreds of thousands of customers of several major organizations.[4]

One major reason for the proliferation of cybersecurity breaches is that the Internet was not designed with security in mind. As noted by Gansler and Lucyshyn (2004, p. 2), "[T]he Internet was designed to share information, not protect it." Recent surveys show that attacks via the Internet are the fastest-growing method of computer crime. In fact, breaches in cybersecurity have been rising at an alarming rate over the past two decades. According to the CERT Coordination Center, which has been collecting data on *security incidents* (events that compromise security) since 1988, the number of security breaches has increased dramatically since 1998.[5] For example, in 1998, CERT reported 3,734 security-related incidents, while in 2003, the number was 137,529.[6] These numbers, however, are only the tip of the iceberg because many, if not most, security breaches are never reported. Additionally, a large number of security breaches go undetected. Equally alarming are the costs associated with cybersecurity breaches. These costs are of both an explicit and an implicit nature.

Business and government leaders now recognize the significance of the frequency and costs of cybersecurity breaches. Today, cybersecurity is at the forefront of discussions about the Internet.

---

[4] See Saranow and Lieber (2005).

[5] Data are from CERT Coordination Center (2004).

[6] Although the CERT definition of a security incident used to generate these numbers has included intrusion attempts on computer systems via the network, there seems to be growing agreement among security professionals that intrusion attempts by themselves do not constitute a security breach.

In early 2004, Microsoft offered a $250,000 reward for information leading to the arrest and conviction of the author of the "MyDoom" computer virus. The magnitude of this reward indicates the scope and seriousness of the problem.

The cost of information security is essentially a negative network externality associated with the Internet.[7] This negative network externality arises when malevolent individuals and organizations join the network, thereby imposing costs on all well-intentioned users. These costs take the form of losses caused by actual security breaches plus the costs of actions (such as purchasing and installing antivirus software) designed to prevent such breaches. For example, the BBC news reported that the cost of the "Code Red" virus in 2001 was estimated to exceed $1.2 billion.[8]

Notice, however, that when an organization installs antivirus software, the newly installed software provides positive spillover effects to the other users of the network. That is, other users of the network receive some of the benefits when one user reduces the likelihood of spreading a virus across the network.

Information value
and its link to security

Information provides value to organizations in numerous ways—by helping managers make better production, marketing, and financing decisions; by helping managers control activities and processes; and by helping to manage the workforce. In today's knowledge-based

---

[7] Camp and Wolfram (2000) liken negative information security externalities to pollution.

[8] See http://news.bbc.co.uk/1/hi/business/1468986.stm.

economy, information assets are replacing physical assets as a means of giving one organization a competitive advantage over another in the marketplace. Given the strategic nature of information, organizations must safeguard this asset as they would physical assets.

Protection of information is essential for facilitating normal day-to-day transactions related to buying and selling in today's digital economy. In order to conduct electronic transactions, digitized information concerning prices, product specifications, and purchasers' payment information must be securely, as well as easily, transmitted. All the e-business models—business-to-business (B2B), business-to-consumer (B2C), and business-to-government (B2G)— rely on the secure transmission and storage of sensitive information. It is essential to establish trust so that buyers and sellers are willing to participate in electronic transactions. Even firms that make all of their sales in traditional brick-and-mortar stores rely increasingly on e-commerce to manage their supply chains. Moreover, at traditional stores, sales personnel enter credit card information into the firm's computer system and electronically transmit this information to banks and credit card companies. Hence, secure information plays a valuable role in nearly all types of day-to-day business transactions.

In addition to information related to normal day-to-day business transactions, wide ranges of other types of information are key strategic assets in today's organizations. Such strategic information includes, but is not limited to, information on secret recipes, products under development, marketing plans, mergers and acquisitions, personnel, and customer demographics. Clearly, such strategic information is crucial to an organization's viability and growth. The value of this information to an organization is inextricably tied to its level of privacy and security.

Organizations typically collect information from other parties based on the understanding that the organization will protect the confidentiality of the information. This is particularly true of financial and medical information. Legal liability and compliance with laws and regulations provide organizations with strong incentives to protect this information.

The threat of litigation arises whenever the (real or perceived) failure of an organization's information security system affects another party. In addition to damage caused by the release of confidential information (e.g., medical records or financial records), damage may also include impairment of another party's computer system (including data, hardware, and software) from passing on a computer virus, libelous statements about another party being made on the organization's (tampered with) Web site, or participating (voluntarily or involuntarily) in a denial-of-service attack that shuts down the Web site of a third party. Investing in information security to comply with current industry practices and legal and regulatory requirements, along with careful documentation of the analysis underlying cybersecurity investment decisions, provides organizations with some degree of protection.

Legal and regulatory requirements vary across industries and tend to be more stringent in some industries than in others. Among those industries with especially strict requirements are the healthcare and financial sectors. Prominent examples of the types of requirements in these industries are the Health Insurance Portability and Accountability Act of 1996 (HIPAA)[9] and the Gramm-Leach-Bliley Act of 1999 (GLBA),[10] which are concerned with protecting

---

[9] For the full text of this legislation, see Health Insurance Portability and Accountability Act (1996).

[10] For the full text of this legislation, see Gramm-Leach-Bliley Act (1999).

the confidentiality of clients' medical and financial records, respectively. Furthermore, as pointed out in the *Wall Street Journal* article referred to previously, several states have passed, and many more are moving toward passing, laws that put a "freeze" on the credit history of consumers.[11] The purpose of these latter laws is to prevent thieves from opening up credit-related accounts based on stolen information (i.e., without a review of a consumer's credit history, most merchants will not open credit accounts for these people).

Security then and now: the rise of information concerns

The Internet dramatically changed the way organizations approach security. In today's world of interconnected networks, the protection of digitized information is at least of equal importance with the protection of physical assets.

To illustrate this point, let us consider security within a bank and imagine that we are back in the year 1960. As the manager of a local bank, you realize that bank robbers exist and that part of your job is to prevent these people from robbing your bank. In other words, you need to provide bank security. Accordingly, you hire a bank guard, make sure that your bank's vault is time-locked, and install hidden buzzers so that employees can contact the police in the event of a robbery. Meanwhile, a specific individual is planning to rob the bank tomorrow. This would-be robber devises a plan that involves walking into the bank and demanding money from customers and bank employees in a traditional "hold-up." In preparation for the robbery, the individual gathers the necessary supplies and resources to carry out the robbery—a weapon (e.g., a handgun), a kit for making disguises, a car for leaving the scene of the

---

[11] Saranow and Lieber (2005).

crime, and a driver for the car. In addition, the robber might, if only briefly, consider the illegality of his plan and the potential for bodily harm to all involved.

Now let us fast-forward to today. A bank manager still faces the possibility of robbery. An individual could still attempt to rob the bank the old-fashioned way, in which case his "tools of the trade" would be quite similar to those of his counterpart in 1960, although the weapon might be more powerful and the car much faster. Alternatively, the robber could pursue a more modern approach, using a computer (possibly from the comfort of his home) to rob the bank via an electronic transfer of funds. This modern approach uses different tools of the trade, eliminates the threat of bodily harm to all parties, involves less risk of apprehension because the criminal could be physically far from the crime scene (perhaps even in a different country), and provides the potential for a significantly larger payoff for the robber because the theft is no longer limited to the cash on hand at the bank.

As a bank manager today, you therefore face a more complex security challenge. Not only do you have to provide security to guard against an old-fashioned hold-up, but you also have to ensure that the information on your bank's computers is secure from a malicious *hacker* (an individual who gains unauthorized access to a computer system). Although not discussed in this example, there are other types of security issues confronting the manager of our hypothetical bank. For example, employee theft is, and always has been, a key security issue.

These scenarios illustrate the changing world that began with the advent of computers and the Internet. Of course, the need to provide cybersecurity is not limited to banks in today's digital economy. Indeed, all organizations (in both the private and public sectors of a country's economy) need to give careful attention to issues related to cybersecurity.

What exactly is cybersecurity?

Cybersecurity involves the protection of information that is accessed and transmitted via the Internet or, more generally, through any computer network. For the purposes of this book, the terms *cybersecurity, computer security,* and *information security* are used interchangeably. The main objectives of cybersecurity, as shown in Figure 1-1, are to (1) protect the *confidentiality* of private information, (2) ensure the *availability* of information to authorized users on a timely basis, and (3) protect the *integrity* (i.e., the accuracy, reliability, and validity) of information. Two additional information security concerns are *authentication* (i.e., making sure that authorized users are who they claim to be) and *nonrepudiation* (i.e., making sure that authorized users cannot deny the fact that they are the actual users). Authentication and nonrepudiation are often treated as a subset of either availability or integrity. For example, the Federal Information Security Management Act (FISMA) of 2002 treats authentication and nonrepudiation as a subset of integrity.

Be aware that the goals of cybersecurity often conflict with one another. For example, requiring authorized users to provide numerous passwords and identifying information can strengthen the confidentiality of private information, but at the cost of reducing the availability of the information in a timely manner. The rope linking the three objectives of cybersecurity in Figure 1-1 highlights the fact that cybersecurity objectives can pull an organization in different directions.

The effectiveness of cybersecurity critically depends on the technical and human resources available to support it. From a technology perspective, organizations need to use the appropriate mix of such resources as encryption techniques, firewalls, access controls, and intrusion detection systems. In addition, people need to know how to use these technical tools properly to prevent information security breaches.

FIGURE 1-1   Main objectives of cybersecurity.

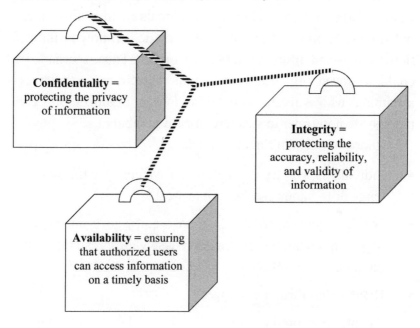

Threats and vulnerabilities

Cybersecurity activities are designed to deal with the threats and vulnerabilities associated with the operation of a networked computer system. *Threats* to an organization's computer information system are the sources of potential actions or events that could cause information security breaches. Threats emanate from nature, individuals, groups, or organizations that deliberately or unintentionally cause an information security breach. Thus, a tornado that could destroy an organization's computer hardware is a threat, as is a criminal who is intent on breaking into an organization's computer system in order to steal credit card numbers.

Other examples of threats include:

- Individuals who try to break into a system only for the challenge or to vandalize, but not to steal

- Foreign agents or terrorists (sponsored by governments or rogue organizations) seeking to cause widespread damage (economic and otherwise) to a country

- Disgruntled former employees

- Agents sponsored by competing firms who are engaging in industrial espionage

These threats all originate from sources external to an organization. There are also threats that originate from sources within an organization. For example, disgruntled and/or careless current employees may be significant potential internal sources of breaches of information security.[12]

---

[12] See Gordon and Loeb (2001a) for a discussion on how threats from competitors interact with information security management. Gordon and Loeb (2003) provides a more formal analysis.

Vulnerabilities are weaknesses in an organization's computer information systems that increase the likelihood of successful attacks on those systems. For example, leaving a laptop computer in an unlocked office rather than a locked office would significantly increase the laptop's vulnerability to the threat of theft. The probability that the laptop would actually be stolen would therefore depend on the presence of threats as well as on the vulnerabilities. Since the value of the asset affects the intensity of the threats, the probability that a laptop would be stolen would be greater if it were an expensive, state-of-the-art computer rather than a four-year-old inexpensive laptop.

Management of cybersecurity

In the early days of computer networks, there was a widespread belief that security was solely a technological problem. As a result, organizations initially emphasized *encryption* (the practice of decoding and encoding messages), so that only legitimate receivers and senders would be able to make sense of the transmitted information. Other technical issues that rapidly surfaced as being of key importance to cybersecurity included firewalls, access controls, and intrusion detection systems. Today, however, business and government leaders recognize that cybersecurity is as much an issue of *management* (i.e., planning, directing, coordinating, and controlling the use of resources to accomplish a given objective) as it is a technical issue.[13]

Since computer security is a relatively new management function, the title and role of the managers responsible for this function differs from organization to organization. In some organizations,

---

[13] What we refer to as a management issue is what some call a business issue.

no management position is dedicated solely to overseeing cyberse-curity. In such organizations, the chief information officer (CIO) is usually responsible for all information technology issues in the organization. For such a manager, information security would sim-ply be one of many responsibilities (including the day-to-day oper-ation of computers and networks, IT training, and the selection of hardware and software).

Some organizations have a chief security officer (CSO) who is responsible for safeguarding all of the organization's assets (physi-cal assets like company automobiles and buildings as well as the data, software, and hardware associated with information technol-ogy). An increasing number of organizations find it useful to desig-nate a chief information security officer (CISO), who has primary responsibility for the firm's cybersecurity.[14] In most organizations, the CISO reports directly to the CIO, although in more and more organizations the CISO reports directly to the chief financial officer (CFO), or even the chief executive officer (CEO).

The manager in charge of information security in the organi-zation, whether given the title of CISO, CIO, or CSO, is responsi-ble for protecting the organization's data and computer systems. The duties of such a manager include developing, coordinating, and implementing the general information security policies for the organization; preparing business contingency plans for recovery from attacks as well as from natural disasters; preparing and pre-senting the business case for cybersecurity investments to the CFO; championing, developing, and implementing information security awareness throughout the organization; and overseeing and training the organization's cybersecurity workforce. The man-ager in charge of information security must be responsive to a

---

[14] Some organizations, especially in the public sector, have designated this person as director of cybersecurity.

number of different stakeholders, including shareholders, regulators, customers, vendors, and business partners.

While an organization's CISO, CIO, or CSO is responsible for the organization's overall information security program, managers further down in the organizational hierarchy must deal with the day-to-day computer security operations. Typically, the person in charge of these computer security operations is the systems administrator. A systems administrator is generally responsible for the complete functioning of the organization's computer system, and security is just one of many responsibilities assigned to this person. Among the security issues that systems administrators address are (1) determining the configuration of hardware and software, (2) implementing access control policies through a password system and/or biometric devices (e.g., hardware and software that check thumbprints to limit access), (3) selecting specific *firewall systems* (software and/or hardware used to prevent unauthorized access to private networks), (4) implementing a system of timely patching of software as vulnerabilities become known, and (5) selecting and operating an *intrusion prevention system* (IPS) and an *intrusion detection system* (IDS). An IPS seeks to prevent breaches by detecting unusual network traffic coming into the system so that the administrator can take suitable preventive actions. An IDS detects security breaches after they have occurred. As such, an IDS alerts managers to successful breaches in order to limit damage and initiate remediation and recovery quickly.

Security standards

Analogous to the development of generally accepted accounting principles (GAAP) in the accounting profession, information security professionals have developed guidelines for information security design and implementation for which they are seeking wide acceptance. In 1996, the National Institute for Standards and Technology (NIST) published SP800-14, "Generally Accepted Principles and Practices for Securing Information Technology Systems," which delineates eight principles that have become known as generally accepted system security principles, or simply GASSP.[15] These principles were originally discussed in the second chapter of the 1995 NIST publication entitled *An Introduction to Computer Security: The NIST Handbook.* The title of this chapter in the handbook is "Elements of Computer Security."

It is interesting to note that the third element discussed by NIST in its handbook is "Computer security should be cost-effective." In 2001, NIST published SP800-27, *Engineering Principles for Information Technology Security (A Baseline for Achieving Security),* which expanded upon the principles and practices put forth in SP800-14 by emphasizing a systems perspective instead of an organizational perspective.[16] The Information Systems Security Association (ISSA) has been overseeing the generally accepted information security principles project, and the current version, entitled "Generally Accepted Information Security Principles (GAISP), version 3.0," available on the Web, is gaining acceptance in the information security community.[17]

Additionally, the International Organization for Standardization (ISO), along with the International Electrotechnical Commission (IEC), issued standard ISO/IEC 17799: 2000, entitled "Information Technology—Code of Practice for Information Security Management." The previous version of this standard was

---

[15] See Swanson and Guttman (1996).

[16] See Stoneburner, Hayden, and Feringa (2001).

[17] See Information Systems Security Association (2004).

ISO 17799, and the standard is commonly referred to by this designation.[18] This standard continues to have substantial global influence, and many organizations have deemed it worthwhile to seek ISO 17799 compliance.

GASSP, GAISP, and ISO 17799 deal with broad guidelines for designing and maintaining information security. There are a number of common themes to these principles and standards. One common theme is that an important tool in managing the risks associated with cybersecurity is the development and implementation of a security policy. A security policy generally includes a statement of the goals of information security, the rules and guidelines for access to computer equipment, acceptable use of such equipment, handling information, data backup, processing information, and acquisition of hardware and software.

Another common theme found in GASSP, GAISP, and ISO 17799 is that of accountability—authority and responsibility for specific information security tasks and activities must be clearly defined. Along with accountability comes access control, whereby access to physical computer hardware or access to specific databases is limited to specific personnel. Still another common theme is that the cost of security should be balanced against the benefits— a key theme of this book. A final example of a common theme in these principles and standards is the need to integrate security measures. Such integration emphasizes coordination, but allows for *defense in depth* (i.e., having multiple layers of protection, such as restricting physical access and requiring passwords).

ISO/IEC 17799, GASSP, and GAISP are frequently incorporated into regulations (including government procurement regulations). Given the legal liability associated with information security

---

[18] "Information Technology—Code of Practice for Information Security Management" is available for purchase. See International Organization for Standardization (2004).

breaches, combined with the growing acceptance of general security principles, CISOs, CIOs, and CSOs face increasing pressure to document compliance with these standards.

Organizations addressing cybersecurity issues

Numerous domestic and international organizations address issues of cybersecurity. Some of these organizations are purely private-sector or purely public-sector organizations. Others have formed alliances across sectors. In the private sector, the Computer Security Institute (CSI) is one of the oldest and a leading organization addressing issues of computer security.[19] Two other well-known private-sector organizations addressing important issues related to computer security are the SANS Institute and the International Computer Security Association (ICSA) Labs (a division of TruSecure Corporation). More recently, the Cyber Security Industry Alliance (CSIA) was formed. CSIA is an advocacy group of software, hardware, and services companies (e.g., Computer Associates International, Inc.; McAfee, Inc.; RSA Security, Inc.; and Symantec Corporation) focused on improving cybersecurity.[20]

The National Association of Corporate Directors (NACD) has also been active in addressing cybersecurity issues, with particular emphasis on the need for information security oversight by corporate boards of directors.[21] Many other professional organizations have played an important role in addressing issues related to cybersecurity issues through their various publications, including the Association for Computing Machinery (ACM), the Institute of Internal Auditors (IIA), the Institute of Management Accountants

---

[19] For more information on CSI, see http://www.gocsi.com.

[20] For more information on the CSIA, see http://www.csialliance.org.

[21] For more information on NACD, see http://nacdonline.org.

(IMA), the Institute of Electrical and Electronics Engineers (IEEE), the American Accounting Association (AAA), and the Information Systems Audit and Control Association (ISACA).

In the public sector, there are several organizations that are actively involved in cybersecurity issues. The most notable U.S.-based organizations are the National Security Agency (NSA), the National Institute of Standards and Technology (NIST), the Government Accountability Office (GAO), the Department of Homeland Security (DHS), and the Federal Bureau of Investigation (FBI).

Several highly visible international organizations are also actively involved in addressing cybersecurity issues, although the scope of these organizations is not limited to cybersecurity concerns. These organizations include the Organization for Economic Co-operation and Development (OECD), the United Nations (UN), and the International Chamber of Commerce (ICC). The OECD, for example, provides "Guidelines for the Security of Information Systems and Networks."

> These guidelines apply to all participants in the new information society and suggest the need for a greater awareness and understanding of security issues, including the need to develop a "culture of security"—that is, a focus on security in the development of information systems and networks, and the adoption of new ways of thinking and behaving when using and interacting within information systems and networks.[22]

The ICC also promotes cybersecurity activities among businesses and governments around the world. In fact, one of the key objectives of the ICC's Commission on E-Business, IT and Telecoms (EBITT) is to "formulate policies on critical telecommunications, information security, data protection and privacy, cybercrime,

---

[22] For more information on the ICC's cybersecurity-related activities, visit http://www.iccwbo.org/home/electronic_commerce/commission.asp.

freedom of communication, international harmonization efforts and jurisdiction and applicable law in e-commerce issues based on a consensus building process."[23]

As discussed earlier, a number of organizations have been involved in developing computer security principles and standards. NIST publications, while directed toward federal government agencies, heavily influence the attitudes and practices in the private sector, and ISSA has taken the lead in developing and promoting information security principles. The ISO, with its 17799 standard, is also quite influential. Finally, the International Information Systems Security Certifications Consortium, Inc. (ISC²), an international not-for-profit organization, is prominent with its certification programs for computer security professionals. The ISC² provides training and examinations for the designation of Certified Information Systems Security Professional (CISSP) and the System Security Certified Practitioner (SSCP).

The standards published by these organizations, as well as other organizations, provide a baseline for cybersecurity. They do not, however, provide enough information to make a spending judgment. The spending judgment issue requires a cost-benefit analysis.

Cost-benefit analysis and cybersecurity

This book presents guidelines for efficiently managing cybersecurity resources based on the economic principle known as cost-benefit analysis. *Cost-benefit analysis* compares the costs of an activity to the benefits of that activity, thereby focusing attention on the process of efficiently allocating scarce resources among competing activities. In the context of cybersecurity, the cost-benefit analysis principle means that one needs to compare the

[23] See the Information Security and Privacy section of the OECD's Web site at http://www.oecd.org/document/42/0,2340,en_2649_34255_15582250_1_1_1_1,00.html.

costs of an additional information security activity with the benefits derived from that activity. As long as the benefits of an additional information security activity exceed its costs, it is worthwhile to engage in that activity. However, if the costs exceed the benefits, one should not engage in that activity. If the costs and benefits of an information security activity are equal, then, technically speaking, one should be indifferent as to whether or not to engage in that activity. Thus, more cybersecurity does not always result in an organization's being better off. This trade-off between the costs and benefits of a cybersecurity activity is illustrated in Figure 1-2.

The benefits associated with cybersecurity activities are derived from the cost savings (often called cost avoidance) that result from preventing cybersecurity breaches. These benefits are difficult, and often impossible, to predict with any degree of accuracy. Moreover, since the actual benefits are conceptually the cost savings associated with potential security breaches that did not occur, it is not possible to measure these benefits precisely after the security investments are made. In fact, the more successful the cybersecurity, the more difficult it is to observe the actual benefits. As a result, many organizations do not use cost-benefit analysis in making resource allocation decisions regarding cybersecurity activities. Some security managers actually argue that using cost-benefit analysis for such decisions is resorting to "voodoo economics." Instead of advocating cost-benefit analysis, it is common for these managers to argue that professional judgment without a formal economic analysis is the preferred method for making resource allocation decisions regarding cybersecurity activities. Although professional judgment is certainly valuable, it is better to view this approach as a complement to, rather than a substitute for, a carefully constructed economic analysis. A number of the organizations that eschew a cost-benefit approach to allocating resources for information security favor a best practices or industry standard approach. Proponents of this

FIGURE 1-2   Costs vs. benefits of additional cybersecurity activity.

A. Benefits exceed (i.e., outweigh) costs, engage in activity

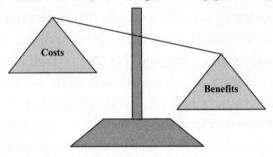

B. Costs exceed (i.e., outweigh) benefits, do not engage in activity

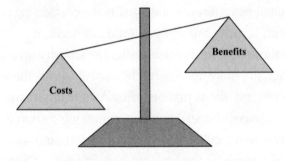

C. Costs equal benefits, be indifferent to the activity

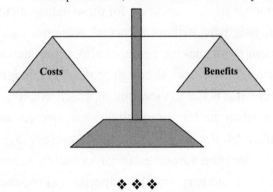

approach argue that it is impossible to measure costs and benefits, and therefore one should just adopt the information security measures that are adopted by a majority of the industry's participants. Such an approach provides managers with a feeling of safety in numbers. The implicit argument underlying this philosophy is usually that the majority is likely to converge toward a "best practices" approach. However, if all firms take this approach, all firms may be either overspending for security or leaving themselves open to unnecessary risks. From a societal perspective, following the majority or best practices approach (or what economists sometimes call *herding*) could be especially dangerous by making a whole industry vulnerable to shutdown from a single threat. Herd behavior may feel good and have some merit, but it is no substitute for carefully conducted analysis.[24] However, from an individual decision maker's perspective, herding may be quite rational under certain conditions.

As argued throughout this book, organizations should use cost-benefit analysis for decisions related to cybersecurity. The fundamental argument is that the management of resources devoted to cybersecurity activities should be based on the economic principle of cost-benefit analysis in a fashion similar to the way in which resources are managed for other organizational activities.

Indeed, we believe that managers in charge of cybersecurity activities who do not embrace this fundamental argument are making a critical mistake in their approach to cybersecurity. In picture form, this argument can be viewed as shown in Figure 1-3. Thus, the basic argument throughout this book is that managers concerned with cybersecurity resources need to be operating in the intersecting area of circles A and B. Of course, this basic argument does not preclude security managers from using professional judgment and/or best practices in tandem with cost-benefit analysis.

---

[24] For an excellent discussion of herding, see Scharfstein and Stein (1990).

FIGURE 1-3   Managing cybersecurity resources.

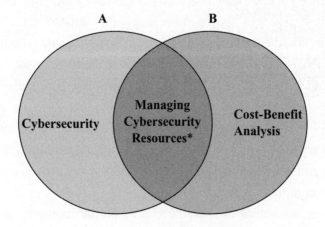

*Managing cybersecurity resources is concerned with managing resources devoted to cybersecurity activities based on the economic principle of cost-benefit analysis.

Cybersecurity myths

A key insight that one should glean from reading this book is that improving cybersecurity requires, in part, debunking some common myths about cybersecurity. More to the point, an important goal of this book is to debunk the five cybersecurity myths listed here. It should be helpful to keep these myths in mind as one reads the remainder of this book.

Myth 1: Cybersecurity activities do not lend themselves to cost-benefit analysis.

Myth 2: All cybersecurity breaches have a significant economic impact on organizations.

Myth 3: Determining the right amount to spend on cyber-security activities is a crapshoot.

Myth 4: The role of risk management in cybersecurity is well understood.

Myth 5: Information sharing has reduced cybersecurity-related problems.

A COST-BENEFIT FRAMEWORK FOR CYBERSECURITY

While economic man maximizes—selects the best alternative from among those available to him; his cousin, whom we shall call administrative man, satisfices— looks for a course of action that is satisfactory or "good enough."

—HERBERT SIMON (NOBEL LAUREATE)[1]

RGANIZATIONS NEED to make resource allocation decisions about cybersecurity activities in a manner consistent with the way resources for other activities within the organization are managed. Cost-benefit analysis is the widely accepted economic principle for managing all of an organization's resources. This principle requires that the costs of an activity be compared to the benefits of the same

---

[1] See Simon (1957), p. xxv. Note that the word *satisfices* appears as it does in the original quote.

activity. When the benefits exceed the costs, it pays to engage in that activity. If the costs exceed the benefits, the opposite is true. When the costs and benefits of an activity are equal, the decision maker should be indifferent to the activity.

This chapter explains the underpinnings of this cost-benefit principle and shows how it provides a framework for managing cybersecurity resources. However, before discussing the cost-benefit aspects of cybersecurity, we first distinguish between operating costs and capital investments.

Operating costs vs. capital investments

The total costs (often called total expenditures) associated with cybersecurity activities can be divided into operating costs and capital investments. *Operating costs* (often called *operating expenditures*) involve expenditures that will benefit a single period's operations, where a single period is usually thought of in terms of one fiscal year. These costs are, in essence, expenses charged to the period. The costs of patching software (including related personnel costs) to correct cybersecurity breaches that occurred this year are an example of operating costs related to cybersecurity activities.

In contrast to operating costs, *capital investments* (often called *capital expenditures*) are expenditures that will benefit an organization's operations for several periods. In other words, unlike operating costs, which are charged as an expense for the period, capital investments represent assets of an organization that should appear on the organization's balance sheet. As capital investments lose their economic value, the portion of the investments that has been lost during a particular period is charged to that period as operating costs. An example of capital investment in cybersecurity activities is the acquisition cost of a new intrusion detection system (including related personnel costs) that is intended to help the organization reduce the likelihood of security breaches for the foreseeable future (e.g., the next two or three years) by detecting attacks on computer systems.

The conceptual distinction drawn here between operating costs and capital investments may seem straightforward. However, in practice, this distinction is anything but straightforward. This is especially true when it comes to discussions of cybersecurity expenditures. Indeed, given the rapidly changing environment associated with cybersecurity activities, many people argue that most cybersecurity expenditures should be treated as operating costs because the benefits derived from such expenditures have a very short life span. In contrast, given that most cybersecurity expenditures have spillover effects to future years, one can effectively argue that nearly all such expenditures should be treated as capital investments. Since both arguments have merit, the best conceptual solution is most likely somewhere in the middle.

In practice, however, organizations tend to treat the bulk of their cybersecurity expenditures as operating costs and charge them to the period in which they are incurred. This generic approach is questionable because, as noted earlier, clearly some of these expenditures should be treated as capital investments. Nevertheless, the accounting and tax rules allow, and even motivate, organizations to treat most expenditures related to cybersecurity as operating costs (i.e., by expensing these costs in the year of the expenditure, tax savings are realized immediately). The fact that corporate balance sheets usually do not explicitly report cybersecurity investments, even though such investments are critical assets for organizations operating in the digital economy, supports the observation that firms generally expense cybersecurity investments.[2]

---

[2] The idea of disclosing cybersecurity investments on the balance sheets of corporations is revisited in Chapter 8.

From a planning perspective, managers should distinguish between operating costs and capital investments in cybersecurity activities, whether or not this distinction is made for financial reporting and tax purposes. Indeed, a good way to view all costs related to cybersecurity activities is to think of them as capital investments with varying time horizons. With this perspective, one can view investments that truly have a one-year time horizon (i.e., those that are truly operating costs) as a special case of the more generic notion of investments. This is the approach we take in this book.

Costs vs. benefits

Recall from Chapter 1 that the three major activities usually associated with cybersecurity are (1) protecting information from unauthorized users of the information, (2) making information available to authorized users on a timely basis, and (3) protecting information from integrity flaws. The costs associated with these activities are often quite substantial. In addition, organizations will incur costs to detect and correct security breaches that could not be prevented. The benefits of cybersecurity are directly related to the cost savings (often called cost avoidance) associated with preventing cybersecurity breaches. We emphasize, however, that no amount of security can guarantee that breaches will not occur.

Let us assume that the anticipated total benefits B and the anticipated total costs C associated with different levels of cybersecurity activities can be assessed. The goal of the organization should be to implement security procedures up to the point where the benefits minus the costs are at a maximum. Implementing cybersecurity activities beyond that point means that the incremental costs are greater than the incremental benefits from the additional security. In other words, the net benefits (i.e., benefits minus costs) from implementing incremental cybersecurity beyond that maximum point are negative. Implementing cyberse-curity activities prior to that maximum point means that the net benefits would be positive if the security procedures were increased to the maximum point.

Following the cost-benefit principle means that the organiza-tion should keep increasing its security activities as long as the incremental benefits from the increase in such activities exceed the incremental costs of those activities.[3] Suppose information security activities could be increased in small increments. Then information security activities should be set at the point where the incremental benefits equal the incremental costs. At this indiffer-ence point, the net benefits are at a maximum.

To illustrate the cost-benefit principle graphically, we assume that the total benefits from cybersecurity activities are increasing at a decreasing rate (i.e., there are diminishing marginal benefits from security activities). We also assume that the total costs asso-ciated with security activities are composed of a fixed portion (costs that do not vary with different levels of cybersecurity activ-ities) and a variable portion (costs that do vary with different levels of cybersecurity activities). For illustrative purposes, the variable costs are assumed to initially increase at a decreasing rate, but eventually increase at an increasing rate. Based on these assumptions, the cost-benefit principle stated earlier is illustrated in panel A of Figure 2-1. As shown in this figure, an organization would invest in cybersecurity activities (SA) up to the point where total benefits B minus total costs C is greatest (SA*), which is the point where the incremental (technically known as

---

[3] An alternative way to view this discussion is to think of the goal as one of trying to min-imize the sum of the costs associated with cybersecurity activities and the costs associ-ated with breaches. Although this is beyond the scope of this book, it can be shown that the optimal level of cybersecurity for an organization would be the same under the cost minimization goal as it would be if the organization were to maximize the net benefits.

FIGURE 2-1   Costs vs. benefits.

**A. Total Costs and Total Benefits in Determining Optimal Level of Cybersecurity
Activities**

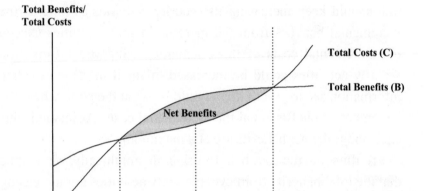

B. Net Benefit in Determining Optimal Level of Cybersecurity Activities

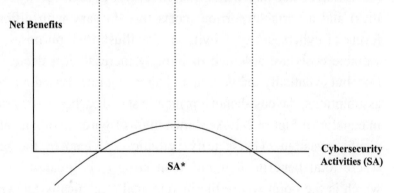

SA* = Optimal Level of Cybersecurity Activities

marginal) benefits equal the incremental (technically known as marginal) costs. The net benefits, which equal the total benefits minus the total costs, are also illustrated in panels A and B of Figure 2-1.

Net present value model

The preceding discussion of costs and benefits can be quantified in terms of a net present value (NPV) model. The NPV model is a financial management tool for comparing anticipated benefits and costs over different time periods. As such, the NPV model is a good way to put cost-benefit analysis into practice. The NPV model begins by discounting all anticipated benefits and costs to today's value, called the *present value* (PV). The difference between the PV and the initial cost of a project is called the *net present value* (NPV). The essence of the NPV approach is to compare the discounted cash flows associated with the future benefits and costs to the initial cost of an investment, where all benefits and costs are expressed in a constant monetary unit (e.g., dollars). In order to simplify the calculations, it is common to assume that the future benefits and costs, with the exception of the cost for an initial investment, are realized at the end of the respective periods.

The NPV model, which is shown in Equation (2-1), is most easily considered in terms of incremental investments. In other words, if we make the rather realistic assumption that some level of cybersecurity is already in place (e.g., basic firewalls and access controls), then managers can use the NPV model to compare the incremental costs with the incremental benefits associated with increases in cybersecurity activities.

$$\text{NPV} = -C_0 + \sum_{t=1}^{n} (B_t - C_t) / (1 + k)^t, \qquad (2\text{-}1)$$

where NPV is as defined above; B_t and C_t are the anticipated benefits and costs, respectively, in time period t from the additional cybersecurity investment; t equals the time period $1, 2, \ldots n$; n equals the number of time periods being considered; C_0 equals the cost of an initial incremental investment; and k equals the discount rate, which is usually assumed to be an organization's average *cost of capital* (i.e., the minimum rate a project needs to earn in order that the organization's value will not be reduced).

The NPV model shown in Equation (2-1) considers the sum of the net benefits in each time period beyond the initial investment. It also allows us to specifically consider an initial up-front investment (i.e., cost), which is represented by C_0 in Equation (2-1). The NPV model provides a simple managerial decision rule for accepting or rejecting incremental cybersecurity activities. This rule is to:

- Accept the incremental cybersecurity activities if the NPV is greater than zero

- Reject the incremental cybersecurity activities if the NPV is less than zero

- Be indifferent to the incremental cybersecurity activity if the NPV equals zero

An NPV greater than zero means that the present value of the anticipated benefits exceeds the present value of the anticipated costs. An NPV of less than zero means that the present value of the anticipated benefits is less than the present value of the anticipated costs. An NPV of zero means that the present value of the anticipated benefits and costs is equal.

A key feature of the NPV model shown here is that it explicitly considers the risk (or uncertainty) associated with benefits and costs. More to the point, the discount rate k used in Equation (2.1) is adjusted to take into account the risk associated with the benefits and costs of cybersecurity activities.

Internal rate of return model

The NPV model provides the basis for a variety of other discounted cash flow models used in financial management. One such derivative model is called the *internal rate of return* (IRR). The IRR, which is often referred to as the *economic rate of return*, equals the discount rate that makes the NPV of the investment equal to zero. Equivalently, the model sets the cost of the initial up-front investment, C_0, equal to the present value of the anticipated future net benefits (i.e., benefits minus costs) and solves for the discount rate that makes them equal [as shown in Equation (2-2)].

$$C_0 = \sum_{t=1}^{n}(B_t - C_t)/(1+\text{IRR})^t,$$ (2-2)

where all variables are defined as noted previously.

Like the NPV model, the IRR model provides a simple managerial decision rule for accepting or rejecting incremental cybersecurity activities. The rule is to:

- Accept the additional cybersecurity activities if the IRR is greater than k (where k is thought of as the organization's cost of capital)

- Reject the additional cybersecurity activities if the IRR is less than k

- Be indifferent to the additional cybersecurity activities if the IRR is equal to k

For individual incremental cybersecurity activities, the decision to accept or reject the activities would be the same under the NPV model and the IRR model (see the examples in the next section). However, if a group of cybersecurity investment opportunities is being considered simultaneously and not all opportunities can be funded, the rank ordering of the opportunities may vary under the two approaches. In general, however, the NPV ranking is preferred to the IRR ranking.[4]

Must-do projects

Some security activities are required by law and therefore must be done irrespective of the NPV or IRR decision rule. These are called *must-do projects*.

A good example of must-do projects is the security investments required to comply with the Health Insurance Portability and Accountability Act (HIPAA) discussed in Chapter 1. According to this act, health-care organizations must "maintain appropriate safeguards to assure that the confidentiality of individuals' health information is properly protected. More specifically, safeguards must be put in place to assure that unauthorized uses or disclosures of the 'protected health information' do not occur."[5] As a result of this HIPAA requirement, health-care organizations need to make information security–related investments in administrative and information systems, irrespective of the cost-benefit aspects of such investments.

The cumbersome nature of the information record keeping required under HIPAA has led many small health-care organiza-

---

[4] For a further discussion of the NPV and IRR models, and other related models such as the probability index (PI) model, see any standard text in economics, finance, or managerial accounting [e.g., Gordon (2004) or Brealey and Myers (2000)].

[5] Health Insurance Portability and Accountability Act (1996).

tions (e.g., small partnerships of medical doctors) to outsource at least part of the requisite security activities in order to minimize the must-do investment. The decision to outsource, however, is merely transforming a must-do capital investment expenditure into a must-do operating expenditure.

Of course, one could argue that many must-do projects are really justified on a cost-benefit basis because of the high penalties resulting from noncompliance with the relevant law. In other words, by avoiding the penalties associated with noncompliance with the relevant law, the cost savings from many, although not all, must-do projects exceed the actual costs of the projects. This fact notwithstanding, the mandatory nature of must-do projects sets them apart from more traditional (i.e., voluntary) cost-saving projects.

Examples

Scenario 1

To see how to apply the basic NPV and IRR models discussed here, let us assume that an organization is considering adding a new intrusion detection system (IDS) to its cybersecurity defenses. As shown in Figure 2-2, the new IDS will involve an initial investment outlay of $200,000. In other words, an initial investment is made at the very beginning of the first period; this is labeled C_0. This investment is expected to have a two-year useful life under this first scenario. It is also assumed that the annual incremental benefits (i.e., the cost savings) generated from the investment will be $400,000 and the annual incremental operating costs associated with the system will be $100,000. Thus, the net benefits (apart from the initial investment) are estimated to be $300,000 per year ($400,000 − $100,000). For simplicity in the discounting process, we make the usual assumption that these annual net benefits (or net savings) are

FIGURE 2-2   Net present value (NPV) and internal rate of return (IRR) calculations investment with two-year useful life: Scenario 1.

A.

Net Present Value (discount rate = 15%)

	C_0	t_1	t_2
Initial investment	−$200,000		
Annual benefits (i.e., cost savings)		$400,000	$400,000
Annual operating costs	_____	−$100,000	−$100,000
Net cash flow	−$200,000	$300,000	$300,000

$$\text{NPV} = -\$200{,}000 + \frac{\$300{,}000}{(1.15)^1} \quad \frac{\$300{,}000}{(1.15)^2}$$

$$\text{NPV} = -\$200{,}000 + \$260{,}870 + \$226{,}843$$

NPV = $287,713

B.

Internal Rate of Return

	C_0	t_1	t_2

$$0 = -\$200{,}000 + \frac{\$300{,}000}{1+\text{IRR}} + \frac{\$300{,}000}{(1+\text{IRR})^2}$$

$$\$200{,}000 = \frac{\$300{,}000}{1+\text{IRR}} + \frac{\$300{,}000}{(1+\text{IRR})^2}$$

IRR = 118.61%

realized at the end of each year. For this type of project, the organization in question uses a 15 percent discount rate (which is equal to its weighted-average cost of capital).

The NPV for this project, as shown in panel A of Figure 2-2, would be computed as follows:

$$NPV = -\$200{,}000 + \$300{,}000/(1.15) + \$300{,}000/(1.15)^2$$
$$= \$287{,}713$$

Thus, the incremental investment in the IDS would be worth making because the NPV of $287,713 is greater than zero.

The IRR for this project would be computed by setting the initial cost of this project equal to the present value of the annual net benefits over the two-year horizon (again, assuming that all net cost savings are realized at the end of each year). As shown in panel B of Figure 2-2, the IRR would be computed by solving

$$\$200{,}000 = \$300{,}000/(1 + IRR) + \$300{,}000/(1 + IRR)^2$$

The IRR for this new IDS would equal 118.61 percent. Since 118.61 percent is greater than the organization's cost of capital of 15 percent, the incremental investment in the IDS would be worth making under the IRR model.

If the IDS investment discussed here is expected to have only a one-year useful life, the NPV would be computed as follows:

$$NPV = -\$200{,}000 + \$300{,}000/(1.15) = \$60{,}870$$

This point is illustrated in panel A of Figure 2-3. Thus, even if this IDS investment has only a one-year useful life, it would still be made because the NPV would still be greater than zero. The IRR for this one-year IDS, as shown in panel B of Figure 2-3, would be computed by solving the following:

$$\$200{,}000 = \$300{,}000/(1 + IRR)$$

The IRR in this case would equal 50 percent, as shown in panel B of Figure 2-3. Since the IRR for this one-year IDS is greater than

FIGURE 2-3   Net present value (NPV) and internal rate of return (IRR) calculations investment with one-year useful life: Scenario 1.

A.

Net Present Value (discount rate = 15%)

	C_0	t_1
Initial investment	–$200,000	
Annual benefits (i.e., cost savings)		$400,000
Annual operating costs		–$100,000
Net cash flow	–$200,000	$300,000

$$NPV = -\$200,000 + \frac{\$300,000}{(1.15)^1}$$

$$NPV = -\$200,000 + \$260,870$$

NPV = $60,870

B.

Internal Rate of Return

	C_0	t_1

$$0 = -\$200,000 + \frac{\$300,000}{1 + IRR}$$

$$\$200,000 = \frac{\$300,000}{1 + IRR}$$

IRR = 50.00%

---

the organization's cost of capital, once again the IDS investment would be made.

Scenario 2

Let us now assume that the initial cost of the investment in the new IDS is $280,000 instead of $200,000. However, we still assume that the annual incremental net benefits are $300,000 per year and are derived at the end of the period. That is, we still assume that the annual incremental benefits (i.e., the cost savings) generated from the new IDS will be $400,000, and the annual incremental operating costs associated with the new system will be $100,000. If the IDS has a two-year useful life, the NPV would be computed as follows:

$$NPV = -\$280,000 + \$300,000/(1.15) + \$300,000/(1.15)^2$$
$$= \$207,713$$

Thus, as shown in panel A of Figure 2-4, the incremental investment in the new IDS would be worth making because the NPV of $207,713 is greater than zero.

The IRR for this project, as shown in panel B of Figure 2-4, would be computed by solving

$$\$280,000 = \$300,000/(1+IRR) + \$300,000/(1+IRR)^2$$

The IRR for this new scenario would be 70.12 percent. Since the IRR is greater than the organization's cost of capital of 15 percent, the investment in the new two-year IDS would be made.

If the new IDS investment noted is expected to have only a one-year useful life (see panel A of Figure 2-5), the NPV would be −$19,130. This is computed as follows:

$$-\$280,000 + \$300,000/(1.15) = -\$19,130$$

Since the NPV in this case is less than zero, the investment would not be made. The IRR in this one-year case, as illustrated in panel B of Figure 2-5, would be computed by solving

FIGURE 2-4   Net present value (NPV) and internal rate of return (IRR) calculations investment with two-year useful life: Scenario 2.

A.

Net Present Value (discount rate = 15%)

	C_0	t_1	t_2
Initial investment	–$280,000		
Annual benefits (i.e., cost savings)		$400,000	$400,000
Annual operating costs		–$100,000	–$100,000
Net cash flow	–$280,000	$300,000	$300,000

$$\text{NPV} = -\$280,000 \quad \frac{\$300,000}{(1.15)^1} \quad \frac{\$300,000}{(1.15)^2}$$

$$\text{NPV} = -\$280,000 \; + \; \$260,870 \; + \; \$226,843$$

NPV = $207,713

B.

Internal Rate of Return

	C_0	t_1	t_2

$$0 \; = \; -\$280,000 \; + \; \frac{\$300,000}{1+\text{IRR}} \; + \; \frac{\$300,000}{(1+\text{IRR})^2}$$

$$\$280,000 = \frac{\$300,000}{1+\text{IRR}} \; + \; \frac{\$300,000}{(1+\text{IRR})^2}$$

IRR = 70.12%

$$\$280,000 = \$300,000/(1 + \text{IRR})$$

The IRR in this case would equal 7.14 percent. Since the IRR is less than the organization's cost of capital of 15 percent, the investment in the new one-year IDS would not be made.

Further thoughts on k

It was noted earlier that the NPV model adjusts for risk via the k (cost of capital) used in the discounting process. That is, the higher the risk, the higher the k. Of course, a higher k also means a lower NPV.

Most corporations use a weighted-average cost of capital in discounting future cash flows from projects.[6] Since corporations generate funds to finance projects through a combination of debt and equity, the weights are usually based on the relative market value of the corporations' debt and equity.[7] Generally speaking, the weighted-average cost of capital would be applied to all projects. However, it is not uncommon for firms to add a premium adjustment to highly risky projects. For example, if a firm's weighted-average cost of capital is determined to be 15 percent (as used in the previous examples), there is no reason why the firm cannot decide to use 20 percent for certain security investments where the cost savings are highly uncertain.

The attractiveness of a security investment opportunity will be directly related to the k used, since higher ks are associated with lower NPVs. Figure 2-6 illustrates this point for the two scenarios discussed in the previous section. Panel A of Figure 2-6 shows the case where the IDS investment is expected to have a two-year useful

[6] There is a very large body of economics and finance literature on the subject of cost of capital. For an excellent review of this literature, the reader is referred to Brealey and Myers (2000).

[7] For an interesting discussion on how providers of debt tend to be more risk averse than providers of equity, see Lajoux and Weston (1999), Chapter 2.

FIGURE 2-5   Net present value (NPV) and internal rate of return (IRR)
calculations investment with one-year useful life: Scenario 2.

A.		
Net Present Value (discount rate = 15%)		
	C_0	t_1
Initial investment	−$280,000	
Annual benefits (i.e., cost savings)		$400,000
Annual operating costs		−$100,000
Net cash flow	−$280,000	$300,000
NPV	$= -\$280,000 \quad + \dfrac{\$300,000}{(1.15)^1}$	
NPV	$= -\$280,000 \quad + \$260,870$	
NPV = −$19,130		

B.		
Internal Rate of Return		
	C_0	t_1
	$0 = -\$280,000 \quad + \dfrac{\$300,000}{1 + \text{IRR}}$	
$\$280,000 = \dfrac{\$300,000}{1 + \text{IRR}}$		
IRR = 7.14%		

life. Panel B of Figure 2-6 shows the case where the IDS investment is expected to have a one-year useful life. A quick look at Figure 2-6 shows that the attractiveness of the IDS discussed under Scenarios 1 and 2 is quite robust for the case where a two-year useful life is assumed. However, the same cannot be said for the one-year case. In fact, a quick look at panel B shows that the IDS under Scenario 2 would have a negative NPV at all points beyond a k of 7.14 percent.

Return on investment

The notion of return on investment is a concept managers often use that is closely related to the IRR. *Return on investment* (ROI) is essentially an accounting concept that is derived by dividing the last period's annual accounting profits (derived from accounting revenues and costs) by the cost of the investment required to generate the profits. Thus, ROI is normally viewed as a historical measure of performance used for evaluating past investments. In contrast, the NPV and IRR are performance measures used to make decisions about potential new investments. Notwithstanding this fact, some decision makers will estimate the anticipated ROI on a potential investment and then use the anticipated ROI as if it were an IRR. However, unlike the IRR, the ROI technically does not consider the time value of money. Accordingly, the ROI will be equivalent to the IRR only under stringent conditions that are unlikely to be met in practice. One critical condition is that the investment must produce a constant return each year in perpetuity. A second condition is that the accounting profits must coincide with cash profits so that the net cost savings in terms of cash flows results in an equal increase in accounting profits. Since these two conditions are rarely met in practice, it is wrong to assume that the expected return on cybersecurity investments is a good proxy for the expected IRR of such investments.

FIGURE 2-6   Relationship between net present value (NPV) and cost of capital (k).

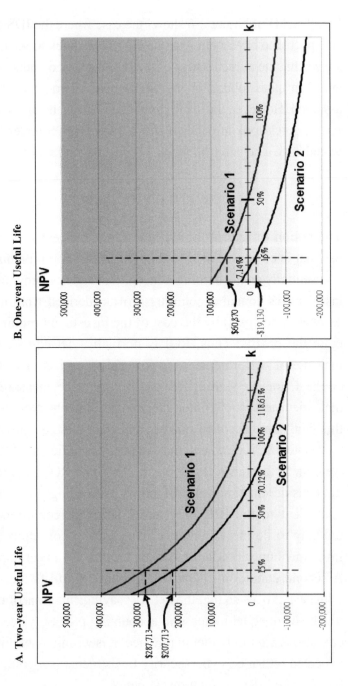

Returning to the previous two scenarios, the determination of the ROI (based on the strict definition of ROI) would not distinguish between the one-year and two-year investments. The ROI for the Scenario 1 investment for both the one-year and two-year cases would be 150 percent, which is derived by dividing the net benefits of $300,000 by the initial investment of $200,000 [i.e., ($300,000/$200,000) × 100%]. The ROI for the Scenario 2 investment, again for both the one-year and two-year cases, would be 107 percent, which is derived by dividing the net benefits of $300,000 by the initial investment of $280,000 [i.e., ($300,000/$280,000) × 100%].

Since the calculation of the ROI implicitly assumes that the investment will continue to produce returns of $300,000 for years 2, 3, 4, and beyond, the ROI dramatically overstates the economic rate of return, the IRR, unless this assumption is correct. The more periods that the returns persist, the better the ROI is as an approximation of the internal (or economic) rate of return.[8] In fact, if the $300,000 net benefit could go on forever, the ROI would in fact be the IRR.

As illustrated previously, ROI is not the same concept as IRR. However, based on a survey of the professional literature in the information security field and conversations with numerous information security managers, clearly many managers are using the ROI acronym to represent the IRR. In other words, they are merely calling the IRR an ROI or ROSI (return on security investment). Given that the concepts of "return on investment" and "internal rate of return" are well established in the accounting, finance, and economics literature, as well as among nearly all senior financial managers (e.g., CFOs), security managers should be careful how they use these terms. Indeed, misusing these terms can only lead to problems for the security manager in his or her quest for a fair share of organizational resources.

[8] For a more comprehensive comparison of NPV, IRR, and ROI in the context of cybersecurity investments, see Gordon and Loeb (2002b).

Financial metrics in practice

Although many organizations resist the use of financial metrics to quantify the cost-benefit aspects of cybersecurity activities, there is growing evidence that suggests that this resistance is waning. For example, recent evidence from the 2004 CSI/FBI survey shows that organizations are embracing the cost-benefit approach to cybersecurity by using the financial metrics discussed earlier.[9] As shown in Figure 2-7, 25 percent of the respondents to the 2004 CSI/FBI survey are using NPV, 28 percent are using IRR, and 55 percent are using ROI.

The trend toward using financial metrics to gauge the cost-benefit aspect of cybersecurity is encouraging. This trend suggests that the recent stream of research related to "the economic aspects of information security" is starting to have an important impact on organizations. However, it must be noted that cost-benefit analysis is often carried out more in line with the spirit of "satisficing" than with truly "maximizing." In other words, on a practical level, decision makers are bounded in their ability to be completely rational in an economic sense. As a result, decision makers have what Simon calls "bounded rationality."[10]

Implications

Information is one of the most valuable assets, if not the most valuable asset, owned by an organization. This is true whether the organization is producing a consumer product for sale in the general marketplace or providing national defense for a country. The Internet accentuates the importance of information to an organization.

---

[9] See Gordon, Loeb, Lucyshyn, and Richardson (2004).

[10] See Simon (1957) for an excellent discussion of the difference between satisficing and maximizing.

FIGURE 2-7   Use of ROI, NPV, and IRR for cybersecurity investments.

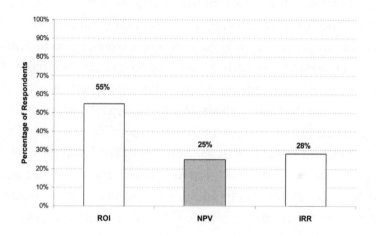

ROI = return on investment

NPV = net present value

IRR = internal rate of return

Source: 2004 CSI/FBI Computer Crime and Security Survey, Fig. 8, Computer Security Journal, *Summer 2004.*

At the same time, the Internet brings with it a rapidly growing problem in the form of cybersecurity breaches. In response to these breaches, a thriving information security industry has emerged.

A large body of research related to the technical aspects of cybersecurity already exists. Much of this research has been effectively applied to organizations. In contrast, there has been very little research focusing on the cost-benefit aspects of cybersecurity. This latter situation is unfortunate because, even if it were technically feasible to keep all computer-based information systems 100 percent secure (which it is not), the costs would be so prohibitive as to render such a remedy unjustified on an economic basis. That is, cost-benefit considerations permeate all aspects of cybersecurity. Thus, in the final analysis, to allocate organizational resources to cybersecurity activities efficiently, the allocation needs to be based on cost-benefit analysis. At the most fundamental level, this means that the economic benefits should exceed the economic costs to justify allocating additional organizational resources to specific cybersecurity activities. This is true whether the organization is a corporation or a government agency. In this latter regard, the idea of applying cost-benefit analysis to the allocation of resources in government organizations is at the heart of a global movement to make government organizations operate more like businesses in the private sector of an economy.

An understanding by cybersecurity managers of how to apply the cost-benefit concept discussed in this chapter can go a long way toward improving cybersecurity within organizations. In other words, *it is a myth to assume that cybersecurity activities do not lend themselves to cost-benefit analysis. The reality is that cost-benefit analysis can, and should, be applied to cybersecurity activities.* The recent trend toward using metrics like NPV and IRR, as shown by the findings from studies like the 2004 CSI/FBI

Computer Crime and Security Survey, suggests that cybersecurity managers are beginning to recognize the potential associated with the cost-benefit concept. Nevertheless, much more attention can and should be given to applying cost-benefit analysis to cybersecurity activities.

THE COSTS AND BENEFITS RELATED TO CYBERSECURITY BREACHES

The costs and benefits of security should be carefully examined in both monetary and nonmonetary terms to ensure that the cost of controls does not exceed expected benefits.

—NATIONAL INSTITUTE OF STANDARDS AND TECHNOLOGY[1]

---

[1] National Institute of Standards and Technology (1995).

THE COMPARISON of costs and benefits is the crux of a sound approach to managing cybersecurity resources. A key portion of cybersecurity costs arises from actions taken to reduce the likelihood of cybersecurity breaches. For example, the expenditures related to implementing firewalls and access controls are part of these costs.

Other critical costs associated with cybersecurity result from the occurrence of actual breaches. These costs include those associated with correcting the causes of breaches, the cost of lost sales, and the cost of legal liabilities resulting from cybersecurity breaches.

Cybersecurity costs also include the costs of precautionary actions taken to mitigate the loss from an information security breach should one occur. The costs of backup storage and redundant systems exemplify this category of costs.

Benefits are cost savings

The benefits derived from cybersecurity activities are essentially the cost savings associated with prevented cybersecurity breaches.[2] Understanding and managing the costs associated with breaches plays a pivotal role in managing cybersecurity resources. We now look at different aspects of managing these costs.

Form and magnitude of cybersecurity breaches

Cybersecurity breaches come in many forms. Some breaches, such as unauthorized access to an individual's financial or medical information, relate to confidentiality. A hacker stealing account numbers from a bank via the Internet would be one example of this

---

[2] Note that a firm may reap additional benefits by gaining a reputation in the marketplace for having cybersecurity that is superior to that of their competitors. Given the game-theoretic nature of this competitive advantage, consideration of this benefit is beyond the scope of this book. See Gordon and Loeb (2003).

type of breach. Highly publicized cases of breaches relating to confidentiality are abundant. For example, in December 2000, hackers attacked Egghead.com's servers and gained access to its customers' credit card information.

Other breaches relate to data availability, such as denial-of-service attacks that prevent access by all (authorized as well as unauthorized) users. The Internet virus called "MyDoom," which closed down many computers during the first few months of 2004, is an example of this type of cybersecurity breach. Yet other breaches jeopardize the integrity of a firm's databases and information systems. A hacker deleting or changing part of a firm's database would be an example of this type of breach.

Cybersecurity breaches not only vary in their form, but also vary greatly in their magnitude. Some breaches affect only part of an organization's information and information systems. Other breaches affect an entire organization or even many organizations (e.g., some viruses, often called worms, can move from one organization to another organization). The value of the information that breaches affect provides another method for ranking the magnitude of breaches. For example, if an unauthorized person has access to a firm's secret formula, that could be far costlier than if a hacker shuts down an organization's Web site for one hour.

Measuring the costs of cybersecurity breaches is no easy task. Yet assessing the economic impact of both actual and potential security breaches is a critical component of securing an organization's computer systems. In fact, managers should determine the appropriate funding of cybersecurity activities, and the appropriate response to actual cybersecurity breaches, based in part on the economic impact of potential and actual cybersecurity breaches.

The prevalence of cybersecurity breaches is well documented. At the same time, there is a large, and rapidly growing, body of literature discussing the costs that result from cybersecurity breaches.

Newspaper and magazine articles on this subject abound. Based on surveys, several studies collect and report out-of-pocket costs resulting from cybersecurity breaches. These studies usually aggregate the total costs from a large number of organizations.

There are also econometric-based studies that have examined the cost of security breaches. These studies tend to focus more on the statistical significance of security breaches than on their absolute dollar value. Furthermore, these studies tend to focus on the economic effect of such breaches on individual organizations.

Even a cursory review of empirical studies makes it clear that security breaches can, and often do, have a serious economic impact on organizations. However, before discussing the empirical evidence about the costs of cybersecurity breaches, let us look at the conceptual issues associated with determining the cost of such breaches. By looking at these conceptual issues, we are able to see the factors affecting the costs and benefits of cybersecurity in a clearer manner.

Direct vs. indirect costs

In order to allocate resources efficiently, managers should distinguish between the direct and indirect costs of cybersecurity breaches. The *direct costs of cybersecurity breaches* are those costs that can be clearly linked to specific breaches. These costs include those associated with the personnel, hardware, and software dedicated to preventing, detecting, and correcting specific breaches. Although direct costs will vary depending on the form and magnitude of a particular cybersecurity breach, the common characteristic of these costs is that they can be traced directly to a particular breach.

In contrast to direct costs, the *indirect costs of cybersecurity breaches* cannot be linked (at least not with any reasonable degree of accuracy) directly to a particular breach. These costs include the overall cost of an intrusion detection system that is used to identify numerous breaches. Although the overall cost of the system can be measured, there is no absolutely correct way to allocate the cost of the system to specific breaches. Thus, to the extent that an accurate allocation of costs to specific breaches will facilitate resource allocation decisions, indirect costs pose an additional challenge for cybersecurity managers. Of course, the problem associated with allocating indirect costs related to cybersecurity breaches is similar to the problem of allocating indirect costs (often called overhead) to different products or services within an organization.[3]

Explicit vs. implicit costs

Managers will also find it useful to separate the costs of cybersecurity breaches into explicit and implicit costs. *Explicit costs of cybersecurity breaches* are those costs of breaches that can be measured in an unambiguous manner. Explicit costs derive from such things as encryption, firewalls, access controls, intrusion detection systems, and other technically oriented cybersecurity activities designed to prevent, detect, and correct security flaws. There are also explicit costs associated with the use of human resources during the design and implementation phases of such activities. In addition, there are explicit costs associated with the development of cybersecurity policies and manuals, awareness training, and cybersecurity audits. Managers can quantify all of these costs in monetary (i.e., financial) terms.

In contrast, *implicit costs of cybersecurity breaches* are *opportunity costs* (i.e., costs associated with lost opportunities), which

---

[3] For a general discussion of the problem associated with allocating indirect costs, the reader should refer to any standard text on managerial accounting [e.g., Gordon (2004)].

cannot be measured without ambiguity. Lost revenues resulting from the negative impact of a cybersecurity breach on a firm's reputation is an example of implicit costs. These costs are often just referred to as a "reputation effect." Another good example would be the potential legal liability that could result from such a breach. The fact that implicit costs cannot be measured without ambiguity leads many to refer to some of these costs as being nonmonetary in nature. Of course, these costs ultimately have a monetary impact, and the goal should be to find ways of quantifying this impact in a manner that permits a meaningful cost-benefit analysis.

Cybersecurity cost grid

The implicit costs associated with cybersecurity breaches often account for the largest share of the real costs of such breaches. Thus, the benefits derived from spending funds on cybersecurity activities come largely from the cost savings derived by avoiding the implicit costs of breaches. Accordingly, any attempt to manage cybersecurity resources needs to consider the differences between implicit and explicit costs. An understanding of the direct vs. indirect cost dichotomy is also important to managing cybersecurity resources.

Figure 3-1 illustrates the conceptual distinction between various forms of cybersecurity breaches and different types of costs. In this figure, we categorize breaches into three types: confidentiality, data availability, and data integrity. The cost dimensions shown in Figure 3-1 are explicit and implicit costs, and also direct and indirect costs. This figure is useful in helping to identify specific costs associated with a particular breach, and we call it a Cybersecurity Cost Grid.

Figure 3-1 is a useful conceptual tool to assist an organization in assessing the costs of cybersecurity breaches. In addition, since

FIGURE 3-1   Cybersecurity cost grid.

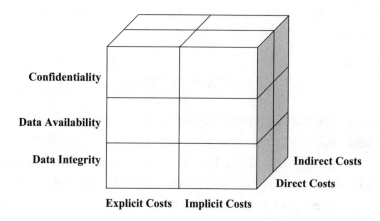

the benefits of cybersecurity activities are derived from the cost savings associated with preventing cybersecurity breaches, Figure 3-1 is a good starting point for assessing the potential benefits of cybersecurity activities. An organization could list potential breaches and their relevant costs for each one of the cells shown in Figure 3-1. The information provided in these cells would provide valuable input for making cybersecurity resource allocation decisions.

Empirical evidence

There is a rapidly growing body of literature providing empirical evidence related to cybersecurity breaches. The Computer Security Institute (CSI) and the U.S. Federal Bureau of Investigation (FBI) conduct one of the most influential, if not the most influential, empirical studies on security breaches. The report resulting from the CSI/FBI survey is published each year in the *Computer Security Journal*. In the 2004 CSI/FBI survey, organizations reported over $141 million in losses resulting from various security breaches.[4]

The losses resulting from security breaches reported by respondents to surveys, such as the one conducted by the CSI and FBI, are only the tip of the iceberg. In fact, experts believe that firms never report the majority of the security breaches that they detect. As noted in the 2004 CSI/FBI study results, the most likely reasons why managers do not report security breaches to law enforcement agencies are concerns over negative publicity and the potential for giving competitors some sort of competitive edge to use against the reporting organization.[5] In addition, some informa-

---

[4] See Gordon, Loeb, Lucyshyn, and Richardson (2004).

[5] Ibid.

tion security breaches go undetected by organizations. As noted in Chapter 1, when aggregated across hundreds of thousands of organizations and individuals, the costs of these breaches can run into the billions of U.S. dollars just from one virus attack, such as "MyDoom" or "Love Bug."

The costs discussed in the previous paragraph relate primarily to the explicit costs of cybersecurity breaches. In reality, however, the implicit costs of security breaches are probably much larger than the explicit costs. Most notable among these implicit costs are the revenues lost as a result of interruptions in business operations and the negative effects on an organization's reputation that result from breaches. In addition, breaches caused by the competitors' espionage activities are another major source of lost revenues. Potential liabilities resulting from breaches of confidentiality are yet another key source of implicit costs.

Unfortunately, it is extremely difficult, if not impossible, to measure the implicit costs of cybersecurity breaches accurately. If the truth be known, the implicit costs of security breaches could probably be in the millions, if not billions, of dollars for one individual organization![6] One approach to measuring these implicit costs for publicly traded corporations is to assess the impact of security breaches on the stock market value of the firms in question. In other words, if information security breaches really do have a significant negative impact on corporations (as the popular press and many survey results suggest), it would be reasonable to expect the stock market to react negatively to publicly announced breaches.

Based on this line of reasoning, we, along with two of our colleagues, conducted an empirical study of the stock market effect

---

[6] The reader should keep in mind that the estimates of billions of dollars in costs for worldwide viruses, such as "MyDoom" and "Love Bug," refer to aggregate losses across hundreds of thousands of organizations and individuals.

of publicly announced breaches. We reported the results of this study in an article in the *Journal of Computer Security.*[7] This study examined the stock market returns of a group of U.S. corporations that experienced security breaches. The breaches examined were publicly discussed in at least one of several highly visible news outlets (e.g., the *Wall Street Journal,* the *Financial Times,* or *USA Today*). As a result of this news exposure, these breaches became well known to the general public. Thus, if security breaches were ever going to have a negative effect on the stock market value of corporations, these highly visible breaches would certainly be good candidates for finding such an impact.

The findings from our study show that, on average, information breaches that compromise confidentiality do have a significant negative impact on the stock market value of corporations experiencing breaches. Indeed, the average decline in the firm's stock market value for cybersecurity breaches associated with confidentiality was approximately 5 percent. To put this percentage into perspective, if a firm had a market value of $100 billion prior to a breach, this would mean that the single breach could cost that one firm around $5 billion in terms of a decline in market value.

In contrast, security breaches that did not compromise confidentiality tended to have a less significant impact on the stock market value of the corporations. In fact, the findings for security breaches of a nonconfidential nature were not economically significant in a statistical sense. These findings suggest that breaches of a nonconfidential nature, although causing firms to incur real losses in an absolute monetary sense, are more like normal operating costs of doing business than like potential financial disasters for most firms. Given the small sample size of

[7] See Campbell, Gordon, Loeb, and Zhou (2003).

the study, it is inappropriate to generalize from the firms included in the study to a larger population. However, further research along similar lines confirms the fact that breaches related to confidentiality do indeed, on average, have the most serious economic impact on the market value of firms. In discussing these findings, it is noted that the "findings are consistent with the intuition that since information security protects a variety of firm assets, the economic consequences of a breach in security depend on the nature and value of the underlying assets compromised by the breach."[8]

We can explain the intuition behind the quote in the previous paragraph by presenting a simple illustration. Assume that before heading off to your job in the morning, you plan to make an electronic transfer of funds from your money market account to your regular checking account. Both accounts are at the same local bank, where you have been doing business for the past ten years. As you are getting dressed, you hear on the radio that your local bank had a computer security breach. Consider the following two scenarios.

Scenario 1

The newscaster reports that a hacker sent your bank a virus that caused the bank's computers to shut down. Furthermore, the newscaster notes that the bank's computers are not expected to be up and running for several hours. In other words, the information security breach causes a denial of service (which is one type of availability breach) to the bank's customers (including you). This event might cause you to get somewhat upset with the bank, but it is unlikely to cause you to contact your bank with the intention of closing out your accounts.

[8] Ibid, p. 445.

Scenario 2

The newscaster reports that your local bank had a computer security breach of a different nature. More to the point, this time the breach involves a hacker's entering the bank's computer systems, acquiring the account numbers of various customers, and transferring money out of some of those accounts. In other words, this time the breach is one of confidentiality. This event may well cause you to contact your bank immediately in an effort to either transfer your accounts to another bank or at least freeze your accounts with the bank in question. In short, your reaction to this breach of confidentiality would probably be significantly different from your reaction to the breach of denial of service.

Implications

The costs associated with cybersecurity breaches are a growing concern to most organizations. These costs are of both an explicit and an implicit nature. Some of these costs can be directly traced to specific breaches, while others can only be indirectly linked to specific breaches.

To the extent that cybersecurity breaches can be traced to flaws in computer software, it is in the best interests of software companies to work toward improving the situation. Indeed, those software companies that produce the most secure products will dominate the competition in the long run. Companies like Microsoft Corporation have recognized this fact and are spending sizable amounts of funds to improve the security of their products. In this latter regard, it is interesting to note that Microsoft's chairman and chief architect, Bill Gates, and its chief executive officer, Steven Ballmer, in their 2004 annual letter to corporate shareholders, address the importance of security. In their words, "a key focus of our innovation is security. Beyond the advances in Windows XP SP2, we are developing advanced technologies that will help isolate computers from Internet attacks and make them more resilient when they are attacked. We are making it easier for customers to keep their systems updated with our latest, most secure software."[9]

The benefits of cybersecurity activities come largely from preventing the costs resulting from cybersecurity breaches. Thus, understanding the cost structure of cybersecurity breaches is essential to the financial management perspective of managing cybersecurity resources in an effective manner. More to the point, cybersecurity managers need to understand how explicit versus implicit costs, as well as indirect versus direct costs, affect the costs associated with security breaches related to confidentiality, data availability, and data integrity.

The empirical findings discussed in this chapter, especially those regarding the effect that information security breaches have on the stock market value of corporations, show that *it is a myth to assume that all cybersecurity breaches have a significant economic impact on organizations. The reality is that a large portion of cybersecurity breaches does not have a significant economic impact on organizations.* However, the cybersecurity breaches associated with confidentiality do indeed tend to have a significant economic impact on organizations. These findings provide some guidance on the way decision makers should manage their cybersecurity resources. More specifically, since 100 percent security for all things is impossible, managers would be wise to allocate a larger share of their organizations' funds to those areas where security breaches can do the most damage. In this regard, cybersecurity managers should pay particular attention to potential security breaches related to confidentiality. Of course, this does not mean that breaches of a nonconfidential nature should be

[9] See Gates and Ballmer (2004).

totally ignored. The fact that security breaches of a nonconfidential nature are not found to be statistically significant for a group of firms and breaches taken as a whole does not preclude the possibility that a particular breach is economically significant for an individual firm (the concept of statistical significance relates to an averaging process, which tends to mask individual effects).

One way to organize the process of allocating resources to particular types of security breaches is to think about potential and actual breaches in terms of the Cybersecurity Cost Grid shown in Figure 3-1. However, as discussed in Chapter 2, in the final analysis, managers should compare the costs and benefits of various cybersecurity activities. This analysis should be linked to the investment and budgeting processes that firms use for allocating funds to cybersecurity activities, the subject of the next chapter.

4

THE RIGHT AMOUNT TO SPEND ON CYBERSECURITY

Not everything that can be counted counts, and not everything that counts can be counted.

—ALBERT EINSTEIN

S WE DISCUSSED in the previous chapter, cybersecurity breaches can, and often do, have a significant negative economic impact on organizations. Thus, managers need to pay close attention to the process of estimating the appropriate amount to invest in cybersecurity activities. Unfortunately, deriving the right amount to invest is both complicated and far from an exact science. These problems notwithstanding, organizations need to address this issue in a rigorous manner.

How much to invest?

The financial management framework discussed in Chapter 2 provides a framework for approaching the question: how much should an organization invest in cybersecurity activities? In essence, this framework tells us that additional investments should be made as long as the benefits of the additional investments exceed the costs of the additional investments. Thus, a good starting point for deciding how much to invest is to consider the potential benefits from such investments.

We know that the benefits from cybersecurity investments come from the "cost savings" associated with the avoidance of potential breaches by engaging in cybersecurity activities. The variables affecting potential cost savings include (1) the potential losses associated with information security breaches, (2) the probability that a particular breach will occur, and (3) the productivity associated with specific investments, which translates into a reduction in the probability of potential losses from breaches of information security.

An intuitive approach for considering these variables is to develop a table that shows the interaction among these variables for different levels of investment. In order to illustrate this approach, consider a simple example involving an investment that has a one-year useful life. Furthermore, assume that all cash flows related to this investment occur at the beginning of the year, so that the time value of money may be ignored. The details of this example are provided in Figure 4-1.

FIGURE 4-1 Example of how much to invest in cybersecurity.

	(1)	(2)	(3)	$(4) = (2) \times (3)$	$(5) = (1) + (4)$	(6)	(7)	$(8) = (6) - (7)$
	Investment Level	Total Potential Loss from Cybersecurity Breach without Investment	Probability of Loss at Each Investment Level	Expected Loss at Each Investment Level	Total Expected Cybersecurity Costs = Investment Costs + Expected Loss from Breaches	Incremental Benefits from Increase in Investment Level (reduction in expected loss, i.e. reduction in column 4 values with additional investment)	Incremental Level of Investment (increase in investment levels, i.e. increase in column 1 values)	Incremental Net Benefit of Increase in Investment Level
A	0	$10,000,000	0.75	$7,500,000	$7,500,000	Not applicable	Not applicable	Not applicable
B	$650,000	$10,000,000	0.50	$5,000,000	$5,650,000	$2,500,000	$650,000	$1,850,000
C	$1,300,000	$10,000,000	0.40	$4,000,000	$5,300,000	$1,000,000	$650,000	$350,000
D	$1,950,000*	$10,000,000	0.33	$3,300,000	$5,250,000	$700,000	$650,000	$50,000
E	$2,600,000	$10,000,000	0.29	$2,900,000	$5,500,000	$400,000	$650,000	-$250,000

* Best level of investment for this example.

69

As shown in Figure 4-1, the organization is contemplating four different levels of investment in cybersecurity technologies (e.g., firewalls, access controls, intrusion detection systems). The alternative investment levels ($650,000, $1,300,000, $1,950,000, and $2,600,000) are shown in the column labeled (1) in Figure 4-1, along with the zero level of investment that represents the status quo. In the absence of any investment, the potential loss from information security breaches is estimated to be $10 million, which is shown in column 2. The probability that such a loss will occur is initially estimated to be 75 percent. However, it is estimated that this probability will decrease to 50 percent, 40 percent, 33 percent, and 29 percent with successive increases in investment in cybersecurity technologies, as shown in column 3.

The total expected cybersecurity costs to the organization are the sum of the investment costs and the expected losses from information security breaches. As the investment level in information security increases, the expected losses from security breaches decrease (see column 4 of Figure 4-1). For the example shown in Figure 4-1, the total expected costs of cybersecurity are smallest at the investment level of $1,950,000, as shown in column 5. Thus, of the choices provided in this example, $1,950,000 is the best investment level.

Another way to determine the best investment level for this example is to focus on the incremental benefits and costs for each investment level. The incremental benefits of increasing the level of cybersecurity investment are shown in column 6 of Figure 4-1. This column shows the decrease in the expected loss from breaches from increasing the investment level beyond the level of the preceding row. For example, looking at the entry in row C, column 6 (C-6), one sees that the incremental benefit of increasing the investment in information security from the $650,000 level to the $1,300,000 level is $1,000,000 (calculated by subtracting the

C-4 entry from the B-4 entry). The incremental costs of increasing the level of cybersecurity investment are shown in column 7 of Figure 4-1 (e.g., C-7 = C-1 less B-1). Column 8 of Figure 4-1 shows the incremental net benefits (i.e., the incremental benefits less the incremental cost of the investment) at each level of computer security investment. The organization is best off increasing the investment level as long as the incremental net benefits are positive. One sees that these net incremental benefits are positive until one reaches the $2,600,000 investment level. The incremental net benefit from investing the last $650,000 is −$250,000 (as shown in column 8). Hence, the organization is best off setting the investment level at $1,950,000, confirming the analysis given in the preceding paragraph.

Although the $1,950,000 investment level is the best solution in this example, it is not necessarily the optimal level of investment. In other words, there are many levels of investments that could be made other than those considered here (e.g., $2,000,000), and the optimal solution would require a listing of all those possibilities. However, from a practical perspective, the simple intuitive approach of considering several discrete investment levels is a useful way for a manager to approach the problem of deriving the optimal level of investment in cybersecurity.

Thus far, we have not needed to compute the net present value (NPV) for this example because we have assumed that the benefits and costs of the cybersecurity investment all occurred at the beginning of the year and therefore are in similar dollars. Nevertheless, the method used in this example is applicable for a general NPV analysis with only a slight modification. To illustrate the NPV analysis, consider the example given in Figure 4-2. This is the same one-year example given in Figure 4-1 with the following two modifications: (1) the benefits from each cybersecurity investment (the reduction in the expected loss from breaches) are realized at the end of the year (while the investment continues to occur at the beginning of the year), and (2) the organization uses a discount rate of 15 percent to evaluate each investment. Using the NPV formula [Equation (2-1)], each incremental investment level could be evaluated separately, where C_0 equals the incremental investment level (the amount invested above the previously analyzed level), B_1 equals the reduction in the expected loss (the cost savings or benefits) resulting from the incremental investment, and $k = 15$ percent equals the discount rate. This is essentially what is done in column 9 of Figure 4-2.

Since the incremental benefits for each incremental investment level occur at the end of the year, they must now be discounted at the 15 percent rate to be properly compared with the incremental costs. The incremental benefit of an investment is the present value of the reduction in expected losses. The present value of the expected loss for each investment level is given in column 5 of Figure 4-2, and the reduction in the present value of the expected loss is given in column 7. The values in column 9 of Figure 4-2 represent the NPV for the additional investment level given in that row. As in Chapter 2, to find the optimal investment level, keep increasing the investment as long as the NPV of the incremental investment is positive. Thus, the best investment level for this second example is $1,300,000. Notice that at this best investment level, the present value of total expected costs (investment costs plus the present value of expected losses from breaches), shown in column 6 of Figure 4-2, are minimized.

In comparing the examples given in Figures 4-1 and 4-2, note that when the time value of money is taken into account, the best level of cybersecurity investment declines from $1,950,000 to $1,300,000. In the example given in Figure 4-2, the benefits of investing occur at the end of the year, and thus are diminished in terms of their present value. Hence, the additional investment of

FIGURE 4-2 How much to invest: incremental analysis using NPV with k = 15 percent.

	(1) Investment Level at $t=0$	(2) Total Potential Loss from Cybersecurity Breaches without Investment at Time $t=1$	(3) Probability of Loss at Each Investment Level	(4) = (2) × (3) Expected Loss at time $t=1$ at Each Investment Level	(5) = (4)/(1+k) Present Value of Expected Loss at time $t=1$ at Each Investment Level	(6) = (1)+(5) Present Value of Total Expected Cybersecurity Costs = Investment Costs + Present Value of Expected Loss from Breaches	(7) Present Value of Incremental Benefits of Increase in Investment Level ($B_1/(1+k)$ = reduction in PV of expected losses, i.e., reduction in column 5 values)	(8) Incremental Level of Investment C_0 (increase in investment levels, i.e., increase in column 2 values)	(9) = (7) − (8) Incremental Net Benefits of Increase in Investment Level (NPV = $B_1/(1+k) - C_0$)
A	0	\$10,000,000	0.75	\$7,500,000	\$6,521,739	\$6,521,739	Not applicable	Not applicable	Not applicable
B	\$650,000	\$10,000,000	0.50	\$5,000,000	\$4,347,826	\$4,997,826	\$2,173,913	\$650,000	\$1,523,913
C	\$1,300,000*	\$10,000,000	0.40	\$4,000,000	\$3,478,261	\$4,778,261	\$869,565	\$650,000	\$219,565
D	\$1,950,000	\$10,000,000	0.33	\$3,300,000	\$2,869,565	\$4,819,565	\$ 608,696	\$650,000	−\$41,304
E	\$2,600,000	\$10,000,000	0.29	\$2,900,000	\$2,521,739	\$5,121,739	\$347,826	\$650,000	−\$302,174

* Best level of investment for this example.

73

$650,000, from the level of $1,300,000 to $1,950,000, produces nominal (i.e., in the absence of discounting) benefits of $700,000 (see D-6 in Figure 4-1) that now have a present value of only $608,696 (see D-7 in Figure 4-2). Hence, this example illustrates how proper discounting can alter cybersecurity investment decisions.

Other potential benefits from cybersecurity investments

For the examples given in Figures 4-1 and 4-2, the only benefit from investing in information security was that the investments reduced the likelihood of security breaches. Investments in cybersecurity may generate benefits other than, or in addition to, lowering the likelihood (probability) of the occurrence of breaches.

One possible type of benefit is a spillover that increases the productivity of other information technology investments. For example, in searching for possible vulnerabilities in proprietary software, IT personnel may discover ways to alter the software to enhance its use. Some cybersecurity investments are not designed to reduce the likelihood of a breach, but rather to reduce the severity of losses if a breach occurs. Investing in an insurance policy with a deductible would fit into this category; if there were a large breach, the organization would be liable only for the deductible. Another example of an investment that lowers the size of the loss from a breach, if one occurs, would be the costs associated with separating customer account information into different files in different locations. While doing so may make accessing the information more costly (or slower), the expected loss associated with certain breaches would be smaller (hackers would obtain less information from a given breach). Note also that this example illustrates the trade-off between protecting the availability of information and increasing the confidentiality of information.

The previous examples looked at only the type of benefit from computer security investments derived from reducing the probability of a breach occurring. Moreover, the method of comparing the (present value of expected) incremental benefits with incremental costs applies equally to all types of investments. In the next section, we generalize the benefits from cybersecurity investments to include a possible reduction in the losses contingent on breaches occurring, as well as a reduction in the likelihood of breaches occurring.

Annual loss expectancy

In 1975, the National Bureau of Standards, the predecessor of the National Institute of Standards and Technology, published Federal Information Processing Standard (FIPS) 65, *Guideline for Automatic Data Process Risk Analysis,* which defined and proposed the *annual loss expectancy* (ALE) approach to measuring information security risk. The ALE measure did not become a formal part of regulatory or procurement standards, and, in fact, FIPS 65 was withdrawn as a guideline in August 1995.[1] Nevertheless, ALE is widely known, and often used, in information security circles.

Unlike the NPV cost-benefit framework discussed earlier, the ALE framework implicitly assumes that the benefits of an information security investment and the costs of the investment do not change from year to year. To understand the ALE framework, we need to introduce some notation.

Suppose that there are n possible breaches that could occur in any one year, and let the index $i = 1, 2, \ldots n$ correspond to each possible breach. Let I_A denote a proposed information security

---

[1] See the National Institute of Standards and Technology's Web site (http://csrc.nist.gov/publications/fips/).

investment (or a particular group of such investments), and let I_{no} represent "no investment" (considered to be the status quo). An information security investment I_A may affect the likelihood (or probability) of a breach occurring in a given year and/or the magnitude of the loss associated with the breach. Let $P_i(I_A)$ be the probability of breach i occurring in a year given an information security investment of I_A, and denote $L_i(I_A)$ as the annual dollar loss that the firm would suffer if the ith breach were to occur when the firm made the I_A information security investment.

The ALE associated with investment I_A may be defined as

$$\mathrm{ALE}(I_A) = \sum_{i=1}^{n} L_i(I_A)P_i(I_A) \qquad (4\text{-}1)$$

where I_A denotes a proposed information security investment, $L_i(I_A)$ is the annual dollar loss that the firm would suffer if the ith breach were to occur when the firm made the I_A information security investment, and $P_i(I_A)$ is the probability of breach i occurring in a year, given an information security investment of I_A. The ALE approach has several weaknesses:

- The ALE measure implicitly assumes that losses, conditional on breaches occurring, remain constant over time.

- The ALE focuses on expected losses and ignores other relevant characteristics of risk, such as dispersion.

- The ALE characterizes the risk of losses that would remain after a given information security investment is made, but it does not provide a rule for choosing the best investment.

- The ALE looks only at the benefit side of security investments and does not compare them with the costs of cybersecurity improvements.

Although the ALE does not incorporate the costs of cybersecurity activities, the ALE approach can be adapted to account for the cost side and be used for determining the amount to invest in information security.[2] To do so, one would first compare the benefit of the investment (over the status quo) with the cost of the investment. Denote the annual cost of the investment I_A as $C(I_A)$. Note that since I_{no} represents the status quo, $C(I_{no}) = 0$. The annual benefit of information security investment I_A would be the reduction in expected loss from breaches: $ALE(I_{no}) - ALE(I_A)$. With the ALE approach, the benefits of an investment are expressed as an annual measure.

Thus, to compare the benefits with the cost of the investment on a comparable basis, one would have to either express the costs of the investment as an annual cost or find the present value of the benefits. For ease of exposition, we denote the cost of the investment I_A as an annual cost, denoted $C(I_A)$. Note that since I_{no} represents the status quo, $C(I_{no}) = 0$. Hence, the net annual benefits of the investment would equal $ALE(I_{no}) - ALE(I_A) - C(I_A)$. The optimal information security investment would be the investment with the highest net annual benefits.

The use of ALE is illustrated in the example in Figure 4-3. For this example, there are four possible intrusions, which, in the absence of new information security investments, would generate annual losses of $1,000,000, $2,000,000, $3,000,000, and $10,000,000 with probabilities of 0.1, 0.05, 0.04, and 0.01, respectively. Thus, the $ALE(I_{no}) = $420,000 [(0.1 \times $1,000,000) + (0.05 \times $2,000,000) + (0.04 \times $3,000,000) + (0.01 \times $10,000,000)]$. Information security investment A has no effect on the magnitude of the losses if the breaches do occur, but it does lower the probability of each of breaches 1, 2, and 3

---

[2] An adaptation of the ALE model for determining the optimal amount to spend on cybersecurity similar to the model that follows can be found in Hoo (2000).

FIGURE 4-3 Annual loss expectancy.

(1) Possible Breaches	(2) Magnitude of Losses without Investment = $L(I_{no})$	(3) Probability of Losses without Investment = $P(I_{no})$	(4) = (2) × (3) Expected Annual Loss from Breach	(5) Magnitude of Losses with Investment A = $L(I_A)$	(6) Probability of Losses with Investment A = $P(I_A)$	(7) = (5) × (6) Expected Annual Loss from Breach	(8) Magnitude of Losses with Investment B = $L(I_B)$	(9) Probability of Losses with Investment B = $P(I_B)$	(10) = (8) × (9) Expected Annual Loss from Breach
1	$1,000,000	0.1	$100,000	$1,000,000	0.05	$50,000	$1,000,000	0.1	$100,000
2	$2,000,000	0.05	$100,000	$2,000,000	0.04	$80,000	$2,000,000	0.05	$100,000
3	$3,000,000	0.04	$120,000	$3,000,000	0.03	$90,000	$3,000,000	0.03	$90,000
4	$10,000,000	0.01	$100,000	$10,000,000	0.01	$100,000	$7,000,000	0.01	$70,000
			$420,000			$320,000			$360,000

ALE (I_{no}) = sum of column 4 items

ALE (I_A) = sum of column 7 items

ALE (I_B) = sum of column 10 items

occurring. As shown in column 7 of Figure 4-3, the ALE of this investment, ALE(I_A), equals \$320,000. Information security investment B has two effects: it lowers the probability of breach 3 occurring, and it lowers the loss associated with breach 4, should that breach occur. Investment B does not affect the probability of breaches 1, 2, and 4 occurring, nor does it lower the magnitude of the losses associated with breaches 1, 2, and 3, should they occur. From column 10 of Figure 4-3, we see that ALE(I_B), equals \$360,000.

Suppose the annual costs of each of investments A and B were \$55,000, i.e., $C(I_A) = C(I_B) = \$55,000$. Then the expected net benefit from investment A would be \$45,000 (= \$420,000 – \$320,000 – \$55,000), and the expected net benefit from investment B would be \$5,000 (= \$420,000 – 360,000 – \$55,000). Thus, with the modified ALE methodology, each investment alternative would be preferred to the status quo, and information security investment A would be preferred to information security investment B. Notice that while ALE has been proposed, and normally referred to, as a risk measure, it does not take into account what one would usually think of as risk. To see this latter point, note that although the ALE-preferred investment, investment A, generates the greatest expected net benefit, it does nothing to reduce the risk to the firm of the consequences of the most damaging breach, breach 4. Many managers would rationally choose information security investment B over investment A, in order to reduce the maximum loss to the firm from \$10,000,000 to \$7,000,000.

GLEIS model

A rigorous mathematical approach to the problem of deriving the right amount to invest in cybersecurity activities, which we call the *GLEIS model*, revolves around the specification and estimation of mathematical security breach functions.[3] These mathematical functions should specify the interactions among the potential loss, the probability that a loss would occur, and the productivity of investments. In essence, the security breach function would mathematically describe the potential cost savings associated with different levels of cybersecurity investments. This approach could also incorporate investments that provide multiyear benefits and costs, as well as consider discounted risk-adjusted cash flows. Thus, this mathematical approach would allow an organization to derive the optimal investment level, but with a significant amount of added mathematical complexity.

Although the mathematical approach to deriving the optimal investment level is beyond the scope of this book, it is worth noting that we were able to derive at least two results that have general implications for a broad range of security breach concerns. First, it is generally uneconomical to invest in cybersecurity activities costing more than 37 percent of the expected loss. In fact, in most cases, an organization would want to invest an amount that is substantially below the one-third rule. The intuition underlying this finding is that as investments in cybersecurity activities increase, there are diminishing marginal returns from such investments. In the simple example in Figures 4-1 and 4-2, that means that the optimal investment (based on a more mathematical approach) would not exceed $2,500,000 (one-third of $7,500,000, representing the expected loss without investment). Our recommendations to invest $1,950,000 for the example given in Figure 4-1 and $1,300,000 for the example given in Figure 4-2 are consistent with this rule.

We can illustrate this first result using a simple one-period version of the GLEIS model with the help of two simple graphs.

---

[3] The GLEIS model is based on the analysis presented in Gordon and Loeb (2002a). See Cavusoglu, Mishra, and Raghunathan (2004) for another economic model characterizing optimal information security investments.

Figure 4-4 illustrates a typical security breach function. Here x represents the amount of expenditure that a firm devotes to information security activities, and $P(x)$ represents the likelihood (i.e., the probability) that there will be a cybersecurity breach during the period. If no resources were devoted to information security, the likelihood of a breach is shown as the y-intercept, $P(0)$. As the resources devoted to cybersecurity activities increase, the likelihood of a security breach diminishes. Notice, however, that the decrease in $P(x)$ is nonlinear— $P(x)$ gets flatter as x increases, reflecting diminishing returns from cybersecurity investments.

Figure 4-5 illustrates the determination of the optimal (i.e., the profit-maximizing) level of information security resources x^* to protect a single information set. If an information security breach were to occur, we assume that the firm would suffer a loss L. The expected benefit from investing x in information security is the reduction in the expected loss equal to $[P(0) - P(x)]L$, as shown in Figure 4-5. The 45-degree line through the origin shows the cost of investing x dollars in cybersecurity. The net expected benefits of the information security investments are shown as the difference between the curves and are maximized at x^*, where the marginal expected benefit from investing a dollar equals a dollar of investment cost. Notice that x^* is far to the left of $P(0)L$, the expected loss in the absence of spending on information security. For broad classes of security breach functions analyzed with the GLEIS model, the ratio of x^* to $P(0)L$ is always less than 0.37, i.e., the firm never wants to spend more than 37 percent of the expected loss on cybersecurity activities.

The second result derived from the mathematical model is that, even for information sets that have the same potential loss from a security breach and face the same threats, organizations should not always direct their cybersecurity investments toward

FIGURE 4-4   Security breach function.

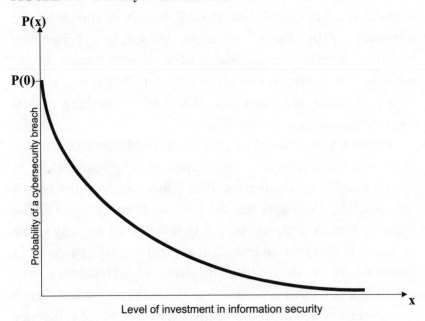

FIGURE 4-5   Benefits and cost of an investment in information security.

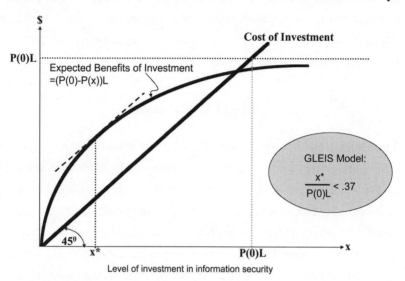

Level of investment in information security

x*: Optimal level of information security investment

those information sets having the greatest vulnerability. The intuition underlying this finding is that some information sets with a high vulnerability are more costly to protect against than the potential cost savings warrants. Thus, an organization may receive a better return on its investment by investing in some cybersecurity activities directed at improving the security of information sets with a medium level of vulnerability.

Budget Constraints

The preceding discussion emphasizes the cost-benefit, or financial management, approach to investing in information security activities. This approach assumes that organizations will continue to invest in cybersecurity activities up to the point where the incremental benefits equal the incremental costs. In reality, however, most organizations have budget constraints that limit the amount they can invest in cybersecurity activities. These budget constraints prevent managers from following the purely economic principle of incremental analysis.[4] Figure 4-6 illustrates this point. In panel A of Figure 4-6, the budget constraint does not affect the optimal security activities. In panel B of the same figure, the budget constraint does affect the optimal security activities.

Budget constraints may be due to growth constraints imposed by senior management. For example, the organization's senior management may believe that growth of more than 20 percent imposes personnel and logistic issues that are not in line with the organization's growth strategy. Another possible reason for budget constraints on investments in cybersecurity activities has to do

---

[4] As organizations increase their investments in cybersecurity activities, it is conceivable that their cost of capital will also increase and thus impose a capital constraint. This type of capital constraint is economic in nature and would be a part of the economic principle of incremental (or marginal) analysis.

FIGURE 4-6   Impact of budget constraint on optimal level of cybersecurity activities.

A. Budget Constraint Does Not Affect Optimal Level of Cybersecurity Activities

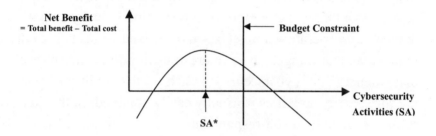

B. Budget Constraint Does Affect Optimal Level of Cybersecurity Activities

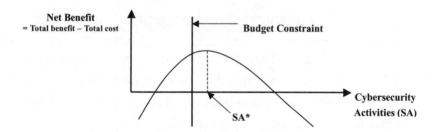

SA* = Optimal Level of Cybersecurity Activities

with organizational politics.[5] In other words, it is quite possible that a politically astute subunit manager (e.g., the head of the marketing department) could get more than her or his fair share of funding than would be justified on a purely economic basis.

Regardless of the reason, it is the rare information security manager who will get whatever funding level she or he can justify based on cost-benefit analysis. In fact, empirical studies have shown that it is common for information security activities to receive an operating budget based on a fixed percentage of the total IT annual budget.[6] It is interesting to point out, however, that when a major cybersecurity breach occurs, additional funding for security activities is usually easily obtained. In this latter regard, over half of the respondents to a survey of major U.S. corporations indicated that actual security breaches resulted in a quick infusion of incremental security expenditures above those initially planned for in the budget.[7] Furthermore, most of the respondents noted that these extra funds were relatively easy to obtain.

Outsourcing cybersecurity

Up to this point, it has been assumed that cybersecurity activities are all done in-house. In reality, however, organizations could outsource some part of these activities (i.e., have an outside organization provide the activities). By outsourcing, an organization is able to take advantage of external expertise, as well as to reduce its initial capital investments (especially those related to hardware, soft-

---

[5] In government organizations, budget constraints are the result of a complicated political process among legislators.

[6] See Gordon and Loeb (forthcoming). The actual percentage used seems to vary widely among organizations.

[7] Ibid.

ware, and personnel). Of course, since the outside organization will charge a fee for its services, the question arises as to whether it is less expensive to outsource than to keep the cybersecurity function entirely in-house. The decision to outsource or keep the function in-house once again comes down to cost-benefit analysis. The basic financial management issue can be thought of as a problem of minimizing the net present value of the costs associated with achieving a given level of cybersecurity. Decisions on whether to make in-house investments for cybersecurity activities or to outsource are similar to what the capital investment literature calls make-or-buy decisions.

As in any make-or-buy decision, one must be careful to focus only on relevant costs and not attribute unavoidable costs solely to the make option. For example, consider the depreciation costs of the portion of a building that is currently allocated to the in-house information security department. Furthermore, suppose that if the information security function were completely outsourced, total depreciation would not change (what would change is the allocation of depreciation to the remaining departments). In this case, the depreciation charge to the information security department is completely unavoidable and should not be added to the in-house (i.e., make) costs of cybersecurity when comparing the in-house cost to the cost of outsourcing.

The quantitative cost-benefit analysis of outsourcing information security should not necessarily be the definitive factor in making the outsourcing decision. Numerous strategic considerations that are difficult to quantify could justifiably sway the decision. These factors include, but are not limited to:

- Differences in the quality of cybersecurity provided

- Desire to maintain the in-house capability to evaluate the quality of cybersecurity

- Concern with sharing confidential information (outsourcing security entails sharing confidential information with the firm providing the cybersecurity, thereby opening the organization to a new threat)

- Spillover benefits from doing the security work in-house (e.g., a network administrator responsible for security as well as operations may learn how to do a better job in operations from the work he or she does on the system's information security)

It is interesting to note that the 2004 CSI/FBI survey results indicate that most organizations do very little to no outsourcing of cybersecurity activities.[8] These findings seem to suggest that the strategic considerations just noted are dominant concerns when it comes to decisions regarding the outsourcing of cybersecurity activities.

Real options and cybersecurity investments

Up to this point, we have implicitly assumed that cybersecurity investments are made either "now" or "never." For a large percentage of cybersecurity investment opportunities, another possibility is to defer the investment to a future date. In other words, if the investment is not made now, it may be possible to make the same investment at a later time (e.g., next year). The ability to postpone an investment is referred to as the *deferment option*. The deferment option is one of a broad class of investment options that economists call *real options*.[9] Like options related to financial securities (e.g., corporate stock options), real options derive their

---

[8] See Gordon, Loeb, and Lucyshyn, 2004.

[9] For an advanced treatment of real options, including the mathematics underlying such options, the reader is referred to the book by Dixit and Pindyck (1994).

value from the fact that the holder can exercise some sort of option related to an asset at a future date. The difference, however, is that in this case the options relate to real (in a physical sense) assets associated with capital investments. The value associated with the deferment option comes from the fact that if an investment is deferred, the uncertainty associated with the investment opportunity will reveal itself in a manner that makes waiting (often called wait-and-see) more rational (in an economic sense) than accepting or rejecting the investment at this point in time.

To see how the deferment option way of thinking applies to cybersecurity investments, consider the following hypothetical example (which ignores the time value of money).[10] Assume that an organization is considering an investment to upgrade the security of all its Internet-related activities. The reason the organization is considering such a cybersecurity upgrade is related to its recent efforts to expand sales over the Internet. Based on company estimates, the newly expanded Internet sales will increase the firm's cybersecurity breaches. The costs associated with these new security breaches (both implicit and explicit costs) are expected to average either $20,000 or $100,000 per month over the next year. The probability that either one of these outcomes will occur is considered to be equal (i.e., there is a 0.5 probability that the extra costs will average $20,000 or $100,000 per month). The cost of the investment, in terms of hardware and software, in the new cybersecurity is expected to be $500,000. By the end of one year, however, it is expected that the technology will change to the point where the $500,000 investment will be obsolete. Thus, the investment will have only a one-year useful life and is assumed to be nonreversible once made (i.e., given the specialized nature of the

---

[10] This example of the deferment option applied to cybersecurity investments is based on the article by Gordon, Loeb, and Sohail (2003).

investment, there is no salvage value associated with it). New cybersecurity opportunities will be considered at the end of the year whether or not the investment currently under consideration is made at this point in time. However, the firm does have the option of deferring the current investment opportunity until next month, at which point the true nature of the increase in security breaches will have revealed itself. That is, after one month the firm will know with certainty whether the extra costs of breaches associated with the new Internet sales are $20,000 or $100,000 per month.

Given these facts, and ignoring the option of deferring this investment, the expected benefits (i.e., cost savings) from the investment in additional cybersecurity activities are equal to $720,000 $\{[(12 \times \$20,000)(0.5)] + [(12 \times \$100,000)(0.5)]\}$. Since the costs of the cybersecurity investment are $500,000, if this is a now or never opportunity, it would pay for the firm to invest in additional cybersecurity. In other words, the benefits from investing exceed the costs by $220,000 ($720,000 − $500,000).

However, now let us assume that this investment could be deferred for one month, by which time the organization will know whether the added security breaches cost $20,000 or $100,000 per month. In this latter situation, the organization would not make the investment in the additional cybersecurity activities if the benefits (i.e., the cost savings) turn out to be $20,000 per month because the remaining benefits would be equal to only $220,000 (11 × $20,000), which is less than the $500,000 investment cost. In contrast, if the remaining benefits turned out to be $100,000 per month, then it would pay to make the investment in one month. In this latter case, the cost savings would be $1,100,000 (11 × $100,000), and this amount exceeds the $500,000 investment cost. The expected benefits from waiting are equal to 50 percent of the difference between $1,100,000 and $500,000, or $300,000, because the probability of the higher cost savings is only 0.5. Therefore, the expected value from deferring the investment is $300,000, which exceeds the $220,000 value from making the investment immediately by $80,000. This $80,000 is referred to as the value of the deferment option. This example is illustrated in Figure 4-7.

The deferment option is only one of several real options that could apply to cybersecurity investments. Another real option that has wide application to cybersecurity investments is sometimes called the strategic option. The *strategic option* refers to the value associated with an investment today that properly positions the firm for the future. In other words, whereas the deferment option relates to the value associated with postponing cybersecurity investments, the strategic option relates to the value that is derived from making an investment today that is related to future events that may surface. For example, the best way for a firm to position itself to address some key cybersecurity issues in the future may be by making some initial cybersecurity investments today—even though these investments do not seem justified on their own merits today. The analysis of strategic options for cybersecurity investments would, in essence, add extra value to today's investment based on potential future events.[11]

Implications

Given that today's organizations derive much of their value from information assets and that these assets face ever-present threats, the need to invest in cybersecurity activities is obvious. The right amount to invest, however, is anything but obvious. Where feasible, managers should derive the right investment level based on the eco-

[11] For a further discussion of strategic options, see Gordon (2004).

FIGURE 4-7 Option value example.

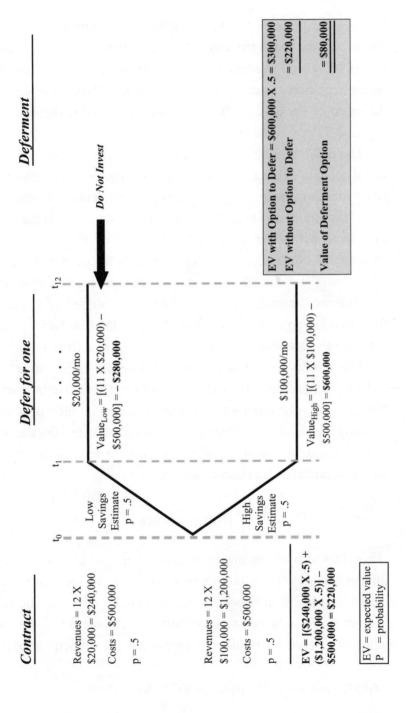

Contract

Revenues = 12 X
$20,000 = $240,000

Costs = $500,000

p = .5

Revenues = 12 X
$100,000 = $1,200,000

Costs = $500,000

p = .5

EV = [($240,000 X .5) +
($1,200,000 X .5)] −
$500,000 = **$220,000**

EV = expected value
P = probability

Defer for one

t_0 t_1 t_{12}

. . . . .
$20,000/mo

Low
Savings
Estimate
p = .5

High
Savings
Estimate
p = .5

Value$_{Low}$ = [(11 X $20,000) −
$500,000] = − **$280,000**

$100,000/mo

Value$_{High}$ = [(11 X $100,000) −
$500,000] = **$600,000**

Deferment

Do Not Invest

EV with Option to Defer = $600,000 X .5 = $300,000
EV without Option to Defer   = $220,000
_____
Value of Deferment Option   = $80,000

nomic concept of cost-benefit analysis. In other words, *it is a myth to assume that determining the right amount to spend on cybersecurity is a crapshoot. The reality is that cybersecurity investments can, and should, be determined in a rational economic manner.* Although an ideal level of investment in cybersecurity activities may not be possible, a meaningful strategy for managers to pursue is to show the benefits derived from investments in cybersecurity activities, both in terms of initially setting the cybersecurity budget and in terms of incremental increases to the budget.[12] This strategy should pay particular attention to issues surrounding cybersecurity risk, which are the focus of the next chapter.

In the final analysis, managers in charge of cybersecurity activities are competing for funds with other managers in the organization (e.g., managers in charge of new product development). Thus, it is imperative for cybersecurity managers to understand how to make the business case (based on cost-benefit analysis) for cybersecurity funds. (Making the business case for cybersecurity funding is the subject of Chapter 6.) It is also imperative for cybersecurity managers to understand how to allocate the funds received in an efficient manner based on financial management concepts. In other words, getting funds for cybersecurity activities is only part of the fiscal task confronting cybersecurity managers. These managers also need to know how to efficiently allocate such funds to competing cybersecurity activities.

---

[12] Although beyond the scope of this book, procedures do exist for combining quantitative concerns with nonquantitative concerns when setting the cybersecurity budget [e.g., see Bodin, Gordon, and Loeb (2005)].

5

RISK MANAGEMENT AND CYBERSECURITY

The superior man, when resting in safety, does not forget that danger may come. When in a state of security he does not forget the possibility of ruin. When all is orderly, he does not forget that disorder may come. Thus his person is not endangered, and his States and all their clans are preserved.

—Confucius

THE NOTION OF RISK plays an important role in allocating resources to cybersecurity. In particular, risk is a key factor when using cost-benefit analysis to determine the right investment level, as discussed in the previous chapter. Unfortunately, risk is a complex concept and is often used to mean different things by different people. The purpose of this chapter is to explain the concept of risk and provide some insights into managing the risk associated with cybersecurity.

Risk metrics

Risk refers to the uncertainty of an event occurring.[1] In the context of cybersecurity, risk usually refers to the uncertainty associated with potentially harmful events occurring. Unfortunately, defining risk is a lot easier than measuring it. This latter point is especially true for the risk associated with a particular set of cybersecurity activities and investments. The best-known risk measure among information security professionals is the expected loss from breaches, which is the measure that provides the conceptual basis for the development and use of the annual loss expectancy (ALE). The expected loss (or, more precisely, the expected value of losses) combines two essential elements associated with risk: the probability of losses and the size of the losses. By summing the product of these two elements, you get the expected loss. In the cybersecurity literature, the expected loss is usually associated with the riskiness of not having enough security. However, there is more to the notion of risk than expected loss.[2]

To see that the expected loss does not capture the whole risk story, let us look at the three cybersecurity investments given in Figure 5-1. Figure 5-1 provides information on three investments, denoted as A, B, and C. Each investment represents a different com-

---

[1] In some of the early economics literature, a distinction is made between risk and uncertainty. Risk in this literature refers to uncertain events that can be characterized by a probability distribution. Uncertainty, in contrast, refers to uncertain events that cannot be characterized by a probability distribution. For purposes of this book, we do not distinguish between risk and uncertainty.

[2] In the economics and finance literature, the expected value is usually not considered a risk metric by itself.

bination of information security activities and technologies, although they are all assumed to cost the same amount. For simplicity, we assume that everything (the losses from the breaches and the expenditures/investments in cybersecurity) takes place in a single period. Furthermore, we assume that there are only four possibilities regarding losses: (1) no breaches will occur, and therefore the loss is zero, (2) breaches resulting in losses of $1,000,000 will occur, (3) breaches resulting in losses of $2,000,000 will occur, and (4) breaches resulting in losses of $3,000,000 will occur. These possibilities are shown in column 1 of Figure 5-1. The probabilities of each level of loss occurring with investments A, B, and C are provided in columns 2, 4, and 6, respectively, of Figure 5-1.

As can be seen from the last three rows of Figure 5-1, information security investments A, B, and C result in the same expected loss from breaches. This expected loss is $1,200,000. Even though all of these investments have the same expected loss, they differ with respect to other measures of risk. This will be demonstrated by considering three additional risk metrics.

The first additional risk metric to consider in the context of cybersecurity is the probability that any loss will occur (or equivalently, for this illustration, the probability that the organization will suffer a loss of at least $1,000,000). By examining columns 2, 4, and 6 in Figure 5-1, we see that using this risk metric, investment B would be deemed to be the least risky, with a probability of a loss of 40 percent (i.e., there is a 60 percent probability of no loss), followed by investment A with a 60 percent probability of a loss (i.e., there is a 40 percent probability of no loss), and investment C would be deemed to be the most risky, with an 85 percent probability of a loss (i.e., there is a 15 percent probability of no loss).

Rather than focusing on the probability that any loss will occur, the second additional risk metric focuses on the probability of the largest losses occurring (i.e., the probability that the organization

FIGURE 5-1 Three cybersecurity investments yielding equal expected losses.

(1) Possible Losses	(2) Probability of Losses with Investment A	(3) = (1) × (2) Expected Value of the Given Loss with Investment A	(4) Probability of Losses with Investment B	(5) = (1) × (4) Expected Value of the Given Loss with Investment B	(6) Probability of Losses with Investment C	(7) = (1) × (6) Expected Value of the Given Loss with Investment C
$0	0.4	$0	0.6	$0	0.15	$0
$1,000,000	0	$0	0	$0	0. 6	$600,000
$2,000,000	0.6	$1,200,000	0	$0	0.15	$300,000
$3,000,000	0	$0	0.4	$1,200,000	0.1	$300,000

Expected value of losses with investment A = sum of column 3 $1,200,000

Expected value of losses with investment B = sum of column 5 $1,200,000

Expected value of losses with investment C = sum of column 7 $1,200,000 will suffer a loss of $3,000,000). By examining Figure 5-1, we see that using this risk metric, investment A would be deemed to be the least risky, with no chance of a $3,000,000 loss, followed by investment C, with a 10 percent chance of a $3,000,000 loss, and investment B would be deemed the most risky, with a 40 percent chance of a $3,000,000 loss.

In the economics and finance literature, the variance is the measure of risk most commonly utilized. Thus, a third additional risk metric to consider in the context of cybersecurity is the variance of the losses. The variance (or the standard deviation, which equals the square root of the variance) is a measure of the dispersion of the associated probability distribution of losses. To calculate the variance, first take the sum of the product of the probability of each loss and the square of the difference between each possible loss and the expected loss. The variance of losses for investment A equals 0.96M (where M stands for millions), the variance of losses for investment B equals 2.16M, and the variance of losses for investment C equals 0.66M.[3] Hence, using variance as a measure of risk, investment C is the least risky, followed by investment A, with investment B being the most risky.

As this example demonstrates, no single risk metric captures all the elements of risk associated with a set of information security activities and investments. While the expected loss metric ranks the riskiness of investments A, B, and C as being equal, the ranking of the riskiness of the three investments was not consistent across the additional three metrics examined. With respect to the first additional metric (probability of any loss occurring), the ranking of investments, from least risky to most risky, was seen to be B, A, C. The ranking with respect to the second additional risk metric (proba-

---

[3] To see where these numbers come from, consider investment C. The variance would equal $0.15(0 - 1.2M)^2 + 0.6(1M - 1.2M)^2 + 0.15(2M - 1.2M)^2 + 0.1(3M - 1.2M)^2 = .66M$.

bility of the largest loss occurring) was seen to be A, C, B. Finally, the ranking of riskiness based on the third additional risk metric (variance of losses) was seen to be C, A, B. Figure 5-2 summarizes these results. Since summary measures cannot capture the many facets of risk, decision makers must consider the entire risk picture (in technical language, the entire probability distribution of losses), as well as their risk preferences (discussed later in the chapter), when selecting among different sets of cybersecurity activities and investments.

Although no single metric summarizes risk, an investment's expected loss from breaches provides all the information needed for a manager who is *risk-neutral* (i.e., a manager who is concerned only with the expected return on an investment). Suppose it were possible for a manager to purchase an information security system for $1,200,000, denoted as system D, that was known to be 100 percent effective in preventing all breaches. Alternatively, suppose the manager could, without any cost, implement any of the three information security systems, A, B, or C, characterized by the losses and probability of losses given in Figure 5-1. By definition, a risk-neutral manager would have no preference among these four choices.

In contrast, a manager who is *risk-averse* (i.e., a manager who prefers an investment with a certain return to one with an uncertain return with the same expected value) would choose the certain investment, D. A risk-averse manager would be expected to always be willing to give up some expected return in order to reduce the risk associated with the return. So, for example, a risk-averse manager who currently has information security system A may be willing to pay up to $1,300,000 for system D, which guarantees that no breaches will occur. In other words, the risk-averse manager is willing to pay $1,300,000 to avoid risks that have an expected loss of $1,200,000.

FIGURE 5-2 **Risk rankings of the three cybersecurity investments.**

	Investments		
Risk metric	**A**	**B**	**C**
Expected value of losses	Same	Same	Same
Probability of any loss	Middle	Lowest	Highest
Probability of the largest loss	Lowest	Highest	Middle
Variance of losses	Middle	Highest	Lowest

The $1,300,000 is known as investment A's *certainty equivalent* (i.e., the certain amount that leaves the decision maker indifferent between the certain amount and the risky return). The certainty equivalent of a particular investment depends on the riskiness of the investment and the decision maker's attitude toward risk. For any risk-neutral investor, the certainty equivalent is the expected value of the return. For a risk-averse security manager, the certainty equivalent will vary from decision maker to decision maker, but will always be greater than the expected value of the investment's return.

Managers can incorporate the riskiness of security investments and their own degree of risk aversion by using certainty equivalents to analyze cybersecurity investments. To illustrate the use of certainty equivalents within a cost-benefit perspective for analyzing cybersecurity investments, consider the example given in Figure 5-3.

Without making an additional investment in cybersecurity, the organization would face losses of $1,000,000, $2,000,000, or $3,000,000 with equal probabilities (see column 2 of Figure 5-3) of 20 percent (and a 40 percent probability of incurring no loss). By investing in information security project E, the organization would face losses of $1,000,000, $2,000,000, or $3,000,000 with probabilities (see column 4 of Figure 5-3) of 15 percent, 10 percent, and 5 percent, respectively (and a 70 percent probability of incurring no loss). Assume that the costs of project E are known with certainty to be $750,000, and, for now, assume that the project is a one-year project. Not investing in the project would yield an expected loss of $1,200,000 (from column 3), and investing in the project would yield an expected loss from breaches of $500,000 (from column 5).

To decide whether or not to make the investment, a manager should compare the additional benefits of the investment with the additional $750,000 costs of the investment. The additional benefits

FIGURE 5-3 Comparison of losses with and without additional cybersecurity investment E. Cost of Investment E = $750,000.

(1)	(2)	(3) = (1) × (2)	(4)	(5) = (1) × (4)
Possible Losses	Probability of losses without Additional Cybersecurity Investments	Expected Value of the Given Loss without Additional Investments	Probability of Losses with Investment E	Expected Value of the Given Loss with Investment E
$0	0.40	$0	0.70	$0
$1,000,000	0.20	$200,000	0.15	$150,000
$2,000,000	0.20	$400,000	0.10	$200,000
$3,000,000	0.20	$600,000	0.05	$150,000
Expected value of losses without additional investments = sum of column 3		$1,200,000		
Expected value of losses with investment E = sum of column 5				$500,000

are the reduction in the certainty equivalent losses. For a risk-neutral manager, the certainty equivalent losses are merely the expected losses. Hence, for a risk-neutral manager, the reduction in expected losses of $700,000 (= $1,200,000 − $500,000) represents the certainty equivalent benefit. A risk-neutral manager should be willing to pay up $700,000 for investment E. Since investment E has a $750,000 cost, a risk-neutral manager should decline to make the investment.

The decision process for a risk-averse manager is more complicated. The manager would first have to determine the certainty equivalent loss for the no-investment option and for the investment E option. These two amounts would be determined by answering the following two questions: (1) "What is the largest certain loss that I would accept rather than face a 20 percent probability of a $1,000,000 loss, a 20 percent probability of a $2,000,000 loss, and a 20 percent probability of a $3,000,000 loss?" and (2) "What is the largest certain loss that I would accept rather than face a 15 percent probability of a $1,000,000 loss, a 10 percent probability of a $2,000,000 loss, and a 5 percent probability of a $3,000,000 loss?"

The answers to these questions represent the certainty equivalent losses, which would be greater than the expected losses. Moreover, the greater the perceived risk of the investment, the greater the deviation between the certainty equivalent loss and the expected loss. If, for example, a manager determined that the certainty equivalent loss for the no-investment option is $1,500,000 and the certainty equivalent loss for information security project E is $700,000, the manager would be willing to pay up to $800,000 for E. Hence, since the cost of E was assumed to be $750,000, the manager would want to go ahead with the project.

To properly account for risk in evaluating multiyear projects, the benefits and costs of the project should be expressed in certainty equivalents prior to discounting them by the cost of capital. Unless the decision maker is risk-neutral, one should not base NPV calculations on expected values. To illustrate the procedure for evaluating a multiyear project, we now suppose that the losses and probability of losses given in Figure 5-3 pertained to a two-year period (after which investment E would have no effect on the probability of losses). For simplicity, we assume that all of the $750,000 cost of project E would be incurred at the beginning of year 1. Let $CE(0)$ be the certainty equivalent loss associated with the no-investment option, and let $CE(E)$ represent the certainty equivalent loss associated with the investment in project E. (We have assumed that the probability distribution of losses will be the same in years 1 and 2, so we do not need to index the certainty equivalents by year.) The net present value of project E, which we denote as NPV(E), would be calculated as

$$\text{NPV(E)} = -750,000 + \sum_{t=1}^{2} \frac{CE(0)-CE(\text{E})}{(1+k)^t} \qquad (5\text{-}1)$$

where k is the discount rate. However, since the numerator in Equation (5-1) is adjusted for risk, the k should be a risk-free rate and not a risk-adjusted rate, as discussed in Chapter 2. More will be said about this point later in the chapter. The decision maker would wish to go ahead with project E as long as NPV(E) > 0.

Risk management process

There are numerous ways to consider risk in evaluating cybersecurity activities and investments. In the NPV model discussed in earlier chapters of this book, risk is usually considered in the context of the discount rate (cost of capital) in the denominator of Equation (2-1). Risk management in the economics and finance literature usually focuses on methods of managing, and more specifically reducing, a firm's cost of capital. Alternatively, some discussions of risk management in the economics and finance literature do address risk management via the process of increasing the certainty equivalent of cash flows shown in the numerator of Equation (2-1). These latter discussions are largely confined to theoretical economic treatments of the subject and are rapidly waning from the literature [in the modern financial economics literature, risk is usually addressed in terms of the discount rate used in the denominator of Equation (2-1)].

Risk management in the cybersecurity literature usually refers to the generic process that is concerned with managing, and more specifically reducing, risk. A term often used to refer to this process is *enterprise risk management* (ERM). Enterprise risk management refers to the overall process of managing an organization's exposure to uncertainty with particular emphasis on identifying and managing the events that could potentially prevent the organization from achieving its objectives. ERM is an organizational concept that applies to all levels of the organization.[4] Consistent with this ERM philosophy, the U.S. National Institute of Standards and Technology (NIST), in its *Handbook on Computer Security*, defines *risk management* as "the process to identify, control, and minimize the impact of uncertain events."[5] Of course, minimizing the impact of uncertain events associated with cybersecurity means that various threats and vulnerabilities, as well as the potential loss from security breaches, need to be considered. The control aspect of risk management means that steps also need to be taken to reduce the potential risk.

---

[4] For an excellent discussion of enterprise risk management, see the report by the Committee of Sponsoring Organizations of the Treadway Commission (2004).

[5] National Institute of Standards and Technology (1995), p. 59.

Figure 5-4 summarizes the process of risk management in terms of cybersecurity risk assessment and control. As shown in Figure 5-4, the first phase in implementing the cybersecurity risk management assessment and control process is to identify the cybersecurity risk confronting an organization. Of course, the specific process for identifying cybersecurity risk will vary depending on the risk metric under consideration. Identifying cybersecurity risk will also vary based on organizational characteristics. However, for most organizations, this identification will at least include such things as determining areas of vulnerability, estimating potential losses, estimating the probability that particular threats will become a reality, and considering the expected value of the loss. More sophisticated analyses by some organizations will try to assess the additional risk metrics discussed earlier.

The second phase in implementing the cybersecurity risk assessment and control process is to ask whether the risk is below the level that is acceptable to the organization. If the risk is below the acceptable level, then one need only continue to implement the cybersecurity risk controls that are already in place (step 7 in Figure 5-4). If the risk is above the acceptable level, the third phase in the process is to reduce the risk via investments in technological means (e.g., installation of firewalls) and/or operational means (e.g., more frequent information security audits to ensure that existing information security policies are being followed). The fourth step in the process is to examine the residual risk after additional investments are incurred. Step 5 is to determine if the risk needs to be reduced further. If so, the sixth step is to consider covering the appropriate residual financial risk through the purchase of cybersecurity insurance. Recent developments with the Internet have led many insurance companies to provide insurance as a hedge against cybersecurity breaches.

FIGURE 5-4   Cybersecurity risk assessment and control.

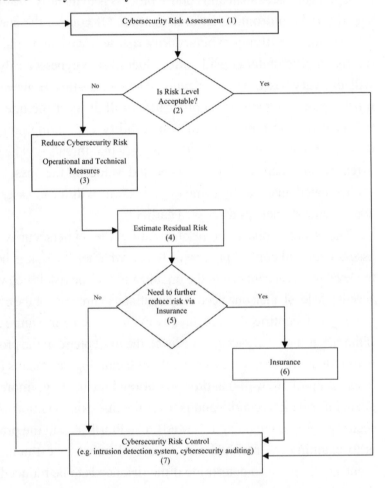

This figure is based on Figure 3 in Gordon, Loeb, and Sohail (2003).

Of course, the goal of maintaining cybersecurity risk at an acceptable level needs to be viewed in cost-benefit terms. That is, the costs associated with incremental reductions in risk (including the cyber-risk insurance) should not exceed the benefits associated with such risk reductions. The seventh, and final, phase of the cybersecurity risk assessment and control process is cybersecurity risk control. Since this is the feedback part of the process, it will lead back into the risk assessment phase, as shown in Figure 5-4.

Implications

Risk and cybersecurity are inextricably related concepts. Underlying this relationship is the notion that risk is directly connected to the exposure and size of a potential loss caused by a cybersecurity breach. As discussed in this chapter, the best-known measure of risk among security managers is derived from the notion of expected losses (i.e., the sum of the product of the various potential losses and the respective probabilities of these losses occurring). Although important, this measure represents only one risk metric. A key implication of the discussion in this chapter is that security professionals need to be familiar with other measures of risk in order to make rational resource allocation decisions concerning cybersecurity activities. Indeed, the focus on expected losses has tended to obscure, rather than clarify, the best way to manage cybersecurity risk. In other words, *it is a myth to assume that the role of risk management in cybersecurity is well understood. The reality is that many cybersecurity managers inadequately understand the full scope of risk management related to cybersecurity.*

In the final analysis, a key concern confronting all organizations is how to manage risk effectively. Managing cybersecurity risk is a process that involves identifying the risk and reducing it to an acceptable level. Of course, the risk management process must also be considered in the context of cost-benefit analysis. That is, it does not make sense to overspend (i.e., spend more than the expected value of the benefits) on any particular stage of the risk management process.

C H A P T E R

THE BUSINESS CASE FOR CYBERSECURITY

Economics has never been a science—and it is even less now than a few years ago.

—PAUL SAMUELSON
(NOBEL LAUREATE IN ECONOMICS)

THE PRIMARY THEME reiterated throughout this book is that organizational resources should be managed based on the general principle of cost-benefit analysis. This is true whether the resources are being applied to cybersecurity or to any other type of organizational activities. Applied to cybersecurity, the cost-benefit principle argues that an organization should keep spending on information security activities as long as the incremental benefits exceed the incremental costs. Furthermore, this argument is applicable to all the security-related pursuits of a firm, including, but not necessarily limited to, computer hardware and software, space facilities, and security-related personnel.

There are many different ways to apply the principle of cost-benefit analysis. The net present value (NPV) model (discussed in Chapters 2 and 4) is one of the most common approaches used to apply the principle. The incremental analysis approach to determining the correct amount to invest in cybersecurity activities (see Chapter 4) is also a derivative of the cost-benefit principle. Rate-of-return models are also derivatives of the cost-benefit principle.

In most large organizations, senior financial executives (e.g., CFOs) require that some form of cost-benefit analysis accompany requests for funds related to capital investments and operating budgets. Although such a requirement has not always been applied to requests for cybersecurity funds, the landscape is clearly changing. That is, there is a growing trend toward requiring cybersecurity managers to compete for resources based on cost-benefit analysis just like other managers.[1]

Consider the following conversation that occurred between the CFO and the senior cybersecurity officer (CO) in a major U.S. corporation at the end of a meeting that lasted close to one hour.[2] "So, my office gets the $7 million investment to upgrade the firm's network security?" asks the CO.

"You haven't made the business case for such an expenditure," replies the CFO.

---

[1] In most organizations, cybersecurity activities, or at least some of these activities, are treated as must-do projects. However, this approach seems to have merit only up to some finite point.

[2] This dialogue is based on an actual conversation between individuals within a major U.S. firm.

In a moment of uncontrolled frustration, the CO says to the CFO, "You do not seem to understand the importance of cybersecurity to our firm!"

At that point, the CFO replies with apparent sarcasm, "You do not seem to understand basic economics and finance." The two individuals agree that another meeting after a two-day cooling-off period would be appropriate.

Empirical evidence suggests that this dialogue, in one form or another, is taking place at many organizations today. For example, the findings from the 2004 CSI/FBI Computer Crime and Security Survey show that a substantial number of organizations are using economic-based metrics like NPV, internal rate of return (IRR), and return on investment (ROI) to justify capital investments in security-related activities. Other empirical evidence confirms the trend toward the use of economic concepts by information security managers in deciding on security-related operating expenditures.[3]

The requirement that economic-based metrics accompany funding requests is usually considered to be an integral part of what is often referred to as "making the business case." As the name suggests, *making the business case* refers to the overall process whereby a proposal is prepared to justify the use of organizational resources in a particular manner rather than other alternative uses of those resources. This process is generic and can apply to operating costs as well as capital expenditures. Nevertheless, the concept is most often associated with capital investments because of the significant impact that such expenditures have on an organization. In fact, in most financial and economics discussions, the term *capital budgeting* is seen as being synonymous with *making the business case*. In this context, capital budgeting

---

[3] The article by Gordon and Loeb (forthcoming) provides an example.

refers to the process by which an organization makes decisions regarding capital expenditures.

In his seminal book on managerial economics, Dean discussed the capital budgeting problem in terms of the following three questions: "(1) How much money will be needed for expenditures in the coming period? (2) How much money will be available? (3) How should the available money be doled out to candidate projects?"[4]

The alternatives that need to be considered in making the business case (or capital budgeting decisions) might span different organizational activities (e.g., a new product line versus increased cybersecurity). The alternatives that need to be considered should also include various options for achieving a given level of cybersecurity, such as the development of sophisticated firewalls versus the development of improved access controls.

Although quantitative (and especially financial) aspects of cost-benefit analysis (e.g., an NPV analysis) usually dominate the general approach to making the business case, nonquantitative concerns also need to be addressed. For example, organizational strategy (the way the organization wants to position itself in the marketplace) needs to be considered. Employee and community relations are other factors that are very important to consider, albeit very difficult to fully quantify, in preparing a business case related to cybersecurity activities.

Business case development

There is an overall process that is generally associated with making the business case (or capital budgeting).[5] Although the details

---

[4] See Dean (1951).

[5] Throughout the rest of this chapter, we will refer to this process as *making the business case*, given the descriptive nature of the phrase. However, the reader should keep in mind that we are using this term as synonymous with *capital budgeting*.

associated with making the business case will vary from situation to situation, the overall process is generic and widely applicable. The four steps discussed here and illustrated in Figure 6-1 provide an overview of this process as it relates to cybersecurity activities. Although these steps are discussed as if they occur in a definitive sequential manner, the arrows in Figure 6-1 are intended to point out that a feedback process can, and usually will, occur. Taken as a group, these four steps represent the planning aspects of managing cybersecurity resources. The control side of cybersecurity resources is discussed in Chapter 7, "Cybersecurity Auditing."

Step 1: Specify Organizational Cybersecurity Objectives

The starting point in making the business case for cybersecurity investments is to clearly specify the objectives (or goals) of such activities. In general terms, the objective is to minimize security intrusions subject to cost constraints. However, organizations must recognize from the start that some cybersecurity breaches will occur. That is, 100 percent cybersecurity (i.e., zero security breaches) is essentially neither technically feasible nor economically rational. Of course, it is important to specify the general cybersecurity objective in more specific and operational terms. This means that cybersecurity managers need to specify the maximum likelihood of breaches that is deemed acceptable for the different classes of breaches. A derivative goal is to continually focus on reducing the maximum acceptable likelihood of breaches over time.

By approaching the cybersecurity objectives in this manner, it is possible to establish benchmarks for the maximum acceptable loss for each class of potential breach (i.e., for breaches related to information confidentiality, integrity, and availability). These benchmarks can then be compared to expected losses from cybersecurity

FIGURE 6-1   Making the business case for cybersecurity
—a process orientation.

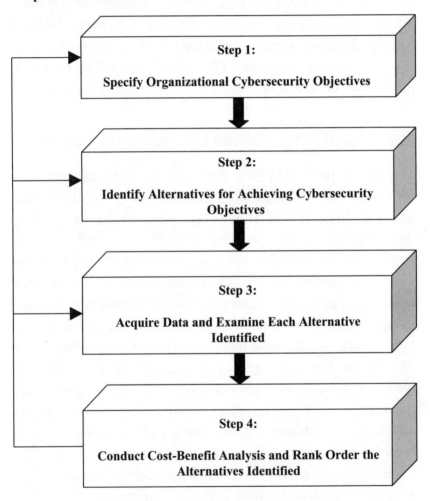

breaches without additional security expenditures. The difference between the benchmarks and the expected cybersecurity losses without additional security expenditures represents the targeted benefits (cost savings) required from additional spending on security. In essence, these targeted benefits represent the minimum objectives of additional cybersecurity expenditures.

Step 2: Identify Alternatives for Achieving Cybersecurity Objectives

Once the objectives related to cybersecurity have been clearly specified, the next step is to identify different ways to achieve those objectives. In other words, this step requires a delineation of the various options available for achieving the cybersecurity objectives specified in the first step. Firewalls, access controls, intrusion detection systems, and appropriate information security personnel are just a few of the alternative means of reducing the likelihood of computer system breaches that need to be considered. For each of these items, there are intra- and interconsiderations. For example, how many and what types of firewalls are available? In addition, consideration should be given to the different combinations of firewalls, access control mechanisms, and/or information security personnel. The trade-off between outsourcing various parts of the organization's cybersecurity activities or keeping them in-house also needs to be identified at this step of making the business case.

Step 3: Acquire Data and Examine Each Alternative Identified

Once the various alternatives have been identified, the next step is to gather the data required to conduct a cost-benefit analysis for each alternative. This step is primarily concerned with delineating the estimates of the various costs and benefits (cost savings) associated with each alternative identified in Step 2. The costs of the cybersecurity for each alternative should be based on the various combinations of cybersecurity activities (e.g., computer networks, firewalls, access control mechanisms, intrusion detection systems, and/or information security personnel). The benefits of each alternative could be estimated by completing a spreadsheet derived from the Cybersecurity Cost Grid illustrated in Figure 3-1. Of course, since the benefits are derived from potential cost savings, the type of cybersecurity employed will directly affect the estimate of such benefits. Thus, the cost grid would need to be completed for different combinations of cybersecurity activities. The potential benefits need to be high enough to ensure that the objectives specified in the first step are met.

Nonfinancial as well as financial information concerning aspects of cybersecurity options should be gathered in this step of developing the business case. For example, organizations need to note the implications of outsourcing key parts of an organization's cybersecurity on employee morale at this step in the development of the business case. Managers should also factor the potential loss of privacy that might result from outsourcing cybersecurity.

Another nonfinancial factor to consider is the maturity of the technology. For some mature technologies (e.g., encryption techniques), where off-the-shelf products are available, the intuitive payoff may be perceived as being much more certain than that for less mature products (e.g., intrusion detection systems, which tend to give a lot of false-positive signals). Of course, the reverse could also be true, in that some products that are less mature may offer the potential for yielding the biggest incremental payoff, thereby justifying more risky investments. The key point here is that the maturity of the technology needs to be considered, one way or the other, in terms of its impact on cybersecurity investment decisions.

Step 4: Conduct Cost-Benefit Analysis and Rank-Order the Alternatives Identified

Once the various alternatives and related data have been clearly identified and gathered, the next step is to conduct the actual cost-benefit analysis and rank-order the various options based on the results of the analysis. This analysis and rank ordering can initially be done in terms of financial concerns. For example, the NPV of the various options could be computed and the ranking could be done in terms of the NPV (i.e., highest to lowest net benefits) for each alternative.[6]

The nonfinancial information gathered in Step 3 should then be used to modify, where appropriate, the purely financial rankings. One way to consider the nonfinancial aspects would be to assign a subjective relative weight to the financial results. For example, a scale of 1 to 7 (with 7 being the highest) could be applied to the various alternatives and multiplied by the financial results.[7]

This step should culminate with a rank ordering of funding priorities and requests for organizational resources related to cybersecurity activities. Since cybersecurity managers are competing for scarce organizational resources, it is unrealistic to expect all cybersecurity activities with a positive NPV to be funded. Thus, a useful

---

[6] The IRR of each alternative could also be computed and used to rank-order options. However, as noted in Chapter 2, this approach is less desirable than rank ordering based on the NPV model.

[7] Although it is beyond the scope of this book, an analytical procedure for combining quantitative and qualitative measures does exist. This procedure is called the analytical hierarchy process (AHP). For an application of AHP to funding decisions concerning information security activities, the reader should see the paper by Bodin, Gordon, and Loeb (2005).

approach would be to attach some overall qualitative measure of security to different levels of funding. For example, at the $4 million request level, the firm's cybersecurity might be judged to be excellent (which is not equivalent to 100 percent security), but at the $3.5 million and $3 million levels, the security level might be assessed to be very good and good, respectively. By assigning different qualitative adjectives to different overall levels of funding, the cybersecurity manager is alerting senior management to the danger of funding below the requested level. For example, funding below $3 million may be deemed unacceptable in terms of meeting the cybersecurity objectives specified in the first step.

The importance of being able to make the business case for cybersecurity expenditures by firms in the private sector has been clearly recognized by senior management at the U.S. Department of Homeland Security (DHS). Indeed, when asked about the commitment of firms in the private sector to spending on security related to protecting the nation's infrastructure, former Secretary of DHS Tom Ridge noted:

> I think we've made great progress with the private sector under the work and through the work of our Information, Analysis and Infrastructure Protection Unit. . . . We have developed a formal means of communication to every sector of our economy and we're in frequent communication, almost daily communication, with one or all of them. We've made great progress across the board in developing a business case so that the kind of investment we expect them to make is viewed as precisely that, not as an expense, but as an investment that has a return that is—you can justify to the shareholders.[8]

The four steps for making the business case are illustrated here in connection with the LarMar Toy Company. This illustration is

---

[8] Comments made by Secretary Tom Ridge at his resignation press conference on November 30, 2004.

based on a combination of several real-world scenarios. However, given the sensitive nature of cybersecurity in most organizations, it does not relate to any particular organization.

LarMar Toy Company

The LarMar Toy Company is a large toy manufacturer with several major subunits, including the New Products Division (hereafter referred to as NPD). NPD is responsible for designing and developing new toys each year. These new toys need to be ready for production by the beginning of the summer, so as to be on the distributors' shelves in plenty of time for the peak toy season, which begins in early November and lasts through the middle of January. Given the competitive nature and short shelf life of new toys, new product development is a highly guarded secret.

The Internet, and more generally computer systems, has created many opportunities for LarMar's NPD in terms of design and development issues, assessing market demand, and dealing with distributors (B2B operations). At the same time, concern about cybersecurity breaches related to confidential information about new products and confidential information about LarMar's distributors has also increased as a result of the increased use of the Internet and other computer-based systems. Thus, the chief security officer (CSO) of LarMar, Ms. Lee, has decided that it is time to upgrade NPD's cybersecurity.

The first step in LarMar's upgrading of its NPD's cybersecurity is to clearly specify the objectives of the upgrade. The key objective of the cybersecurity upgrade is to improve the confidentiality of the information related to the design and development of LarMar's new products, including the interactions related to these new products that LarMar has with its distributors and suppliers. Although 100 percent security in this area is deemed unrealistic, protecting the confidentiality of information related to new toys is a critical concern for LarMar. Given that LarMar's economic viability is dependent on the revenue generated by new toys each year, it is decided that the objective is to reduce the vulnerability of the overall cybersecurity system to a level that could be termed "excellent" (e.g., no greater than 1 percent probability of a security breach). Anything above a 1 percent probability of a security breach is deemed "unacceptable." The next two steps in developing the business case for LarMar's upgrade in cybersecurity related to new products are to identify the alternatives for accomplishing the desired upgrade, and to gather and examine the appropriate data for each alternative.

The current state of cybersecurity related to new products is viewed as being "good" (i.e., there is less than a 10 percent chance of a major security breach), but not good enough. Without any upgrade in the cybersecurity activities, it is estimated that the potential annual loss from a major cybersecurity breach would cost the firm $10 million. Compared to the current situation, the upgrade in cybersecurity for information related to new products should benefit LarMar by providing an annual expected cost savings in the neighborhood of $900,000 for each of the next two years. This expected cost savings is derived by multiplying the annual estimated cost of information security breaches related to new products of $10,000,000 by the 9 percent decline in the probability of such a breach occurring (i.e., going from a 10 percent to a 1 percent probability). After two years, the entire cybersecurity system for new products will be reevaluated in light of the historical evidence on security breaches and the security-related technology available at that time. In other words, this cybersecurity project has a two-year useful life.

After consultation with her staff and NPD's senior management, Ms. Lee decides that two alternatives are worthy of further exploration for meeting the NPD's cybersecurity objective. Each one of these alternatives is expected to lower the probability of a security breach to 1 percent or less. These alternatives are described here and identified in Figure 6-2.

The first alternative for accomplishing the objectives of Lar-Mar's cybersecurity upgrade for the NPD consists of an in-house (hereafter called Alternative I) upgrade of security, including two new cybersecurity staff members. The second alternative for accomplishing the same objectives consists of outsourcing (hereafter called Alternative O) the additional cybersecurity. If the outsourcing alternative is chosen, it is assumed that the cybersecurity company providing the service would be the same one that is already doing some limited information security work for LarMar.[9]

The estimated annual costs for Alternative I are $400,000 in the first year and the second year, paid out at the end of the respective years. These costs include a $250,000 employment package (salary plus fringe benefits) for the two new cybersecurity employees.

Alternative O will result in annual payments of $350,000 (also assumed to be paid out at the end of each year of the two-year agreement). The company being considered for the outsourcing has its headquarters in the same country as LarMar. Thus, the privacy issues discussed in the popular press regarding outsourcing security to firms in foreign countries do not directly surface as a result of this outsourcing alternative.[10] Nonetheless, outsourcing security in lieu of doing it in-house does raise additional privacy

[9] If the outsourcing alternative were put out for bid from various cybersecurity companies, it would be necessary to determine the terms of the outsourcing contract chosen before comparing Alternative I to Alternative O. In other words, it would be necessary to first decide on the best outsourcing option. Of course, if the company chosen for outsourcing were not the one with which LarMar was already doing business, then the security policies of the firm would have to be carefully evaluated.

[10] Outsourcing to firms in foreign countries raises a whole host of political, privacy, and legal concerns apart from the economic considerations.

FIGURE 6-2   LarMar Toy Company: making the business case process.

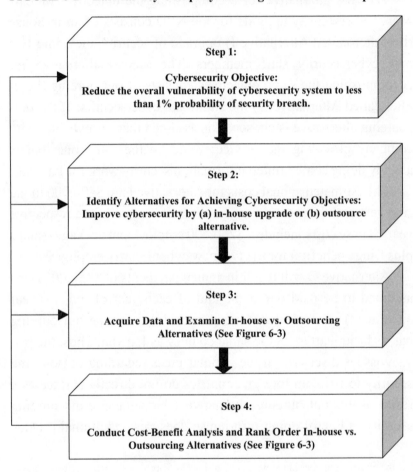

concerns, as well as morale issues with LarMar's CSO and her current staff. For example, outsourcing security raises issues by the very fact that employees of another firm now have access to LarMar's new product information. In addition, if information security on new products is outsourced, LarMar would be well advised to find out the outsourcing policies of the firm to which its security is being outsourced. As a result of examining these additional concerns, it is decided that the outsourcing alternative will be considered based on 75 percent of the annual cost savings (i.e., 75 percent of $900,000 = $675,000). This adjustment to the cost savings is admittedly subjective, but it addresses important concerns and is deemed necessary by Ms. Lee.

The final step in developing the business case for LarMar's upgrade of its cybersecurity related to information on new products is to conduct a cost-benefit analysis and ranking of the two alternatives under consideration. The cost-benefit analysis for each alternative is provided in Figure 6-3. As shown in that figure, the in-house alternative has an NPV of $812,854, and the outsourcing alternative (using the cost savings adjustment) has an NPV of $528,355. These calculations are based on the assumption that LarMar uses a weighted-average cost of capital of 15 percent for evaluating these types of projects. It should be noted that each of the alternatives provides LarMar with a positive NPV. However, assuming that an adjustment to the cost savings is made for outsourcing (i.e., the cost savings are reduced by 25 percent), the in-house alternative ranks above the outsourcing alternative because its NPV is higher. Thus, the decision is to upgrade the cybersecurity of NPD via in-house resources. In other words, the in-house alternative is ranked higher than outsourcing.

Figure 6-3 also shows the calculation for outsourcing under the assumption that a cost savings adjustment is not required. The NPV in this latter case is $894,140. If this were deemed the

FIGURE 6-3   LarMar Toy Company: Cost-benefit computations.

In House Alternative
$$NPV = \frac{(900{,}000 - 400{,}000)}{(1 + 0.15)} + \frac{(900{,}000 - 400{,}000)}{(1 + 0.15)^2}$$
$$= \$812{,}854$$
Outsource Alternative
With Cost Savings Adjustment
$$NPV = \frac{(675{,}000 - 350{,}000)}{(1 + 0.15)} + \frac{(675{,}000 - 350{,}000)}{(1 + 0.15)^2}$$
$$= \$528{,}355$$
Without Cost Savings Adjustment
$$NPV = \frac{(900{,}000 - 350{,}000)}{(1 + 0.15)} + \frac{(900{,}000 - 350{,}000)}{(1 + 0.15)^2}$$
$$= \$894{,}140$$
Ranking of Alternatives
(assuming Cost Savings Adjustment
to Outsource Alternative)
1. In House Alternative
NPV = \$812,854
2. Outsource Alternative
NPV = \$528,355

appropriate analysis, then the outsourcing alternative for the upgrade in cybersecurity would rank higher than the in-house alternative because its NPV is higher. In this case, the decision would be to outsource the cybersecurity upgrade for NPD. This latter calculation highlights the importance of the adjustment process in selecting LarMar's best alternative for cybersecurity. If desired, LarMar could conduct a sensitivity analysis of the appropriate cost savings percentage adjustment to use. Such an analysis would allow LarMar to see at what point the two alternatives are equal.

Implications

The need to allocate scarce resources is a fundamental issue that affects all organizations. As a result, managers from different subunits within an organization usually find themselves competing with one another for these scarce resources. For most organizational activities, competing for resources boils down to what is often called making the business case for funds.

A rapidly growing trend in many organizations is to require cybersecurity managers to compete for funding with other managers (e.g., the new product development manager). In fact, once an organization gets past the basic must-do cybersecurity projects, having cybersecurity managers compete with other managers for additional resources is economically rational. If cybersecurity managers are to be successful in this endeavor, they need to understand how to make the business case for their funding requests. Cybersecurity managers who cannot make a convincing business case for a satisfactory level of organizational resources will eventually fall by the wayside and, more importantly, do a poor job of meeting their organization's needs for cybersecurity. Furthermore, because of the interconnectivity of organizations in the cyberspace world, these managers will have a negative impact on other organizations. Thus, it is in everyone's best interest for organizations to bring their cybersecurity managers up to speed in terms of making the business case for cybersecurity activities.

7

CYBERSECURITY
AUDITING

*Thus it is said that one who knows the
enemy and knows himself will not be
endangered in a hundred engagements.
One who does not know the enemy but
knows himself will sometimes be victorious,
sometimes meet with defeat. One who
knows neither the enemy nor himself will
invariably be defeated in every engagement.*

—SUN TZU, *ART OF WAR*

C YBERSECURITY IS concerned with protecting information that is accessed and transmitted via the Internet. It is best thought of as a planning and control process designed to accomplish the following three key objectives: (1) protect the confidentiality of private information, (2) ensure the availability of information to authorized users on a timely basis, and (3) protect the integrity of information. Once the security process is set in motion, it becomes important to evaluate how well these objectives are being met. This evaluation (control) process is what we call cybersecurity auditing.

Feedback control process

Cybersecurity auditing is a control (monitoring) process for assessing and correcting existing security flaws. As shown in Figure 7-1, cybersecurity auditing completes the planning and control process associated with allocating cybersecurity resources. Cybersecurity auditing not only facilitates corrective actions on existing plans, but also helps to improve the next period's cybersecurity planning by identifying residual security risks associated with vulnerabilities and threats. In some discussions, control is referred to as *post auditing*.[1]

The extent of cybersecurity auditing should vary depending on the organization's business operations, security risks, and size. In general, however, the scope of cybersecurity auditing should usually cover such issues as evaluating the physical security and access controls, verifying administrative procedures and controls, evaluating the effectiveness of the organization's intrusion detection system, and assessing the organization's computer security personnel (including management). In the final analysis, the focus of the cybersecurity audit should be on assessing the economic benefits from information security activities relative to the costs required to conduct such activities.

In many organizations, a checklist of security procedures is prepared, and the audit process involves going through the checklist to evaluate the status of security. The strength of approaching cybersecurity auditing from a checklist perspective is that it does a good job of ensuring that the administrative procedures associated

---

[1] See Gordon (2004).

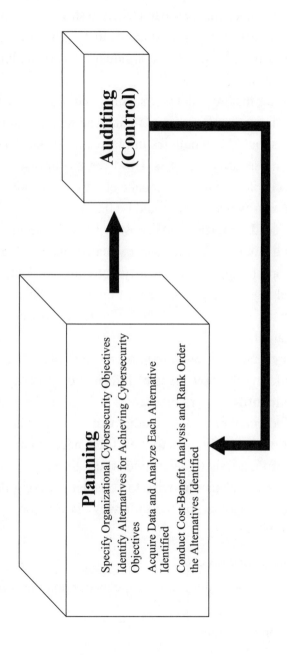

FIGURE 7-1 Cybersecurity planning and control process.

Planning

Specify Organizational Cybersecurity Objectives

Identify Alternatives for Achieving Cybersecurity
Objectives

Acquire Data and Analyze Each Alternative
Identified

Conduct Cost-Benefit Analysis and Rank Order
the Alternatives Identified

Auditing
(Control)

Feedback

with maintaining and improving security are properly carried out. However, the checklist approach tends to shift attention away from the cost-benefit aspects of such security. That is, the checklist approach usually assumes that conducting a particular procedure is inherently worth doing.

Ensuring that certain cybersecurity administrative procedures and activities are in place is important, to be sure. For example, organizations should have policies in place and response teams ready to deal with security breaches. However, as our discussions in the previous chapters of this book make clear, the overriding constraint on cybersecurity activities should be the cost-benefit rule (benefits should exceed, or at least equal, costs). The cybersecurity audit also provides the opportunity to assess whether the cost-benefit rule is being properly applied to security activities. In fact, we believe that checking to see if cost-benefit analysis is being used for all cybersecurity activities should be an important aspect of the cybersecurity audit.

The cybersecurity audit requires an audit plan. The plan begins by considering the objectives of information security, and it also needs to identify the organization's security risks and the dollar value of potential breaches. In other words, since it is not economically rational to audit all activities, there needs to be some sort of cost-benefit analysis to determine where to put your audit funds. As a first pass, it may be wise to consider focusing the audit, to one degree or another, on the following six categories of concern regarding IT security:

1. Policies and procedures
2. Operational and technical aspects of computer hardware and software
3. Personnel-related issues

4. Vulnerabilities and threats

5. The estimated cost of security breaches

6. The payoff derived from information security investments

Within each of these categories, a further refinement is necessary. For example, questions like the following could be asked: Which system violations should be evaluated? What is the organization's access control strategy? Which, if any, personnel are not subject to internal controls? Of course, the security audit will ultimately have to assess the way cybersecurity activities are managed by senior security staff members.

Empirical evidence

Empirical evidence suggests that most organizations do conduct information security audits. For example, the findings from the 2004 CSI/FBI Computer Crime and Security Survey indicate that over 80 percent of organizations conduct such audits. Although most organizations tend to perform security audits at regular, periodic intervals (e.g., once per year), there is a trend toward continuous or "real-time" security audits. Under a continuous auditing process, security audits can be used to continuously improve the security activities based on audit findings. In other words, real-time auditing facilitates a continuous monitoring and corrective action cycle.

Advances in intrusion detection systems have greatly expanded the feasibility of continuous security auditing. Unfortunately, there are usually added costs associated with the added benefits of continuous versus periodic security auditing. These costs can be quite high if the audits are intended to consider the net economic benefits of cybersecurity activities rather than just considering the administrative and physical attributes of security.

Penetration Testing

A commonly used auditing technique for assessing the vulnerability of an organization's computer networks is referred to as penetration testing. *Penetration testing* consists of hacking into one's
own computer network. Penetration tests can be conducted by
internal employees of the organization and/or be outsourced to an
auditing or security consulting firm. The key, however, is to make
these intrusions simulate real attacks. Indeed, the more realistic the
penetration approach, the more helpful it is to those responsible
for maintaining security.

The wide acceptance of the idea of security penetration testing
suggests that most organizations find it to be a value-added security auditing activity. In most organizations, senior security managers are made aware of the fact that penetration testing is going to
occur. However, in some organizations, a senior executive (e.g., the
CFO or CEO) authorizes penetration testing without notifying any
of the firm's security personnel. The senior executive of one major
corporation utilizing this latter approach recently told the authors of
this book that "our information security personnel were shocked
to see how easily our computer networks could be compromised
by the external firm hired to breach our systems." Although the
results were not used for punitive purposes, major changes to this
firm's cybersecurity activities were made as a result of the firm's
penetration testing program.

Agency Problems

Classical economics assumes that managers behave in a manner that
is consistent with the best interests of the firm's owners. Over the
past couple of decades, advocates of agency theory have seriously

challenged this assumption. According to *agency theory*, principals (e.g., the owners of a firm) contract with agents (e.g., the managers of the firm) to make decisions on their behalf. In return, principals reward agents for their performance, which is in part derived from the effort level of the agents.

The first impediment to this contracting process is the fact that agents usually have more information than is normally available to their principals. In other words, there is an asymmetry of information between principals and agents. The second impediment is that there is often a conflict of interests between principals and agents. In other words, agents (e.g., senior managers) are often more concerned with their own economic welfare than with the economic welfare of their principals (e.g., the owners of firms).

The combination of asymmetric information and conflict of interests frequently motivates agents (e.g., managers) to make decisions that are not in their firm's best interests. This situation is referred to as an *agency problem*. For example, some agents will consume excessive nonfinancial perquisites (e.g., lavish offices and artwork) even though this reduces the overall profits of their firms. In order to reduce agency problems, principals set up incentive mechanisms designed to align the agents' interests with those of the principals. Incentive mechanisms take many forms, but those based on an outcome (e.g., a firm's performance) metric are quite common. For example, a bonus plan for senior managers based on a firm's profits is one such mechanism. Stock options offered to the senior managers is another example of an incentive mechanism designed to reduce agency problems. Although they are intended to help align the interests of the senior managers and the owners of firms, stock options have managed to create their own set of problems. In fact, the use of stock options has been linked to many of the accounting scandals of the late 1990s. As a result, the accounting rules governing the use of stock options have gone through a major change throughout the world.[2] Managers who are in charge of the information security of firms can be considered agents who are empowered to make decisions on the part of principals. In this case, the principals (the ones who empower these cybersecurity managers to make decisions) are usually senior-level managers within the firm (e.g., the firm's CIO or CFO). Of course, agency problems can arise between these principals and these agents. For example, information security officers have an incentive to request more funding than is justified on a cost-benefit basis because of the fact that they are the ones who are most likely to suffer damaging career effects when security breaches occur. Incentive mechanisms could be used to resolve this agency problem, such as providing bonuses to security managers who are considered to be performing in a cost-effective manner.

Of course, measuring the cost-effectiveness of security activities raises a whole set of new issues. However, by auditing the process used to measure the cost-effectiveness of security activities, the cybersecurity audit can play a crucial role in enforcing any such incentive mechanisms and thereby reducing agency problems.

Enhancing the firm's value

Cybersecurity auditing can enhance a firm's value in at least two generic ways. First, the mere fact that a firm has such a process in place signals to the managers in charge of IT security that they will be held accountable for their decisions and actions regarding such activities. In other words, the managers in charge of cybersecurity activities now know that there will be a settling-up process that links their actual performance to their expected performance.

---

[2] The change has been toward expensing the value of stock options on a firm's income statement.

Although it is not a panacea for preventing all security problems, this settling-up process can be a strong motivator in making sure that managers will strive to anticipate and resolve information security–related issues. To the extent that security vulnerabilities can be anticipated or detected through penetration testing, it is possible to prevent, or at least minimize, successful attacks. In addition, this settling-up process gives cybersecurity managers a strong incentive to have in place procedures for quickly resolving security concerns that arise.

The second generic way in which cybersecurity auditing can enhance a firm's value is through its ability to serve as a "change agent." In other words, the fact that auditing will take place implies to security managers that actual information security can very well differ from planned cybersecurity. The differences between the actual and planned cybersecurity can serve as a basis for making changes in the way the firm plans, executes, and monitors future cybersecurity activities. In other words, cybersecurity auditing is an integral part of the managerial planning and control process. As such, cybersecurity auditing signals to managers that cybersecurity is a dynamic process that is of critical concern to the organization.

The fact that cybersecurity auditing can enhance a firm's value does not mean that it will always do so. In fact, for some firms, it is quite possible that the costs of cybersecurity auditing will exceed the benefits. If this were to occur, then cybersecurity auditing would in effect decrease the firm's value. Thus, it is important for firms to identify the circumstances under which cybersecurity auditing activities are most beneficial and to determine the appropriate level of such auditing activities (more is not always preferred to less). The limited empirical evidence that exists on this issue indicates that the greater the degree of disparity of cybersecurity-related information between those controlling the purse strings (e.g., the CFO) and those spending the money on cybersecurity activities (the security managers), the more valuable the cybersecurity auditing. This information disparity is called *asymmetric information*.

Implications

Like all organizational activities, cybersecurity activities involve a process of planning and control. Cybersecurity auditing is part of the control side of this process. Managers need to understand the potential benefits of cybersecurity auditing and how it fits into the process, both in general and in terms of their specific organization. Although not a guarantee of a firm's success, an effective cybersecurity auditing program can help managers create net value (have benefits exceed costs) for their firms.

We know that most organizations conduct some form of information security auditing. However, the focus tends to be on the administrative procedures for security. Although these procedures are clearly important, this focus usually misses the economic aspects of cybersecurity auditing. To be most effective from an economic perspective, cybersecurity auditing needs to focus on the cost-benefit aspects of security activities. That is, cybersecurity auditing should incorporate a formal cost-benefit analysis into the various cybersecurity procedures and activities being conducted by a firm. At the same time, to ensure that cybersecurity auditing is a value-enhancing activity, the cost-benefit rule also needs to be applied to the cybersecurity auditing activity itself.

CYBERSECURITY'S ROLE IN NATIONAL SECURITY

Securing cyberspace is an extraordinarily dif-
ficult strategic challenge that requires a coor-
dinated and focused effort from our entire
society—the federal government, state and
local governments, the private sector, and the
American people.

—GEORGE W. BUSH[1]

THE FIRST SEVEN CHAPTERS OF THIS BOOK present a comprehensive argument for using cost-benefit analysis during the process of efficiently managing cybersecurity resources. Up to this point, this argument has intentionally avoided any discussion of the events that have come to be known as the 9/11 attacks. However, we would be remiss not to discuss the impact of this watershed event on the way cybersecurity interacts with *national security* (i.e., protection of the security of a nation), as well as the management of cybersecurity resources.

[1] White House (2003b).

National security

On the morning of September 11, 2001 (hereafter referred to as 9/11), the world watched the unfolding of one of the worst terrorist attacks ever carried out in modern times. Two hijacked airplanes crashed into the Twin Towers of the New York World Trade Center, another hijacked airplane crashed into the U.S. Pentagon, and a fourth airplane, headed for Washington, DC, crashed into a field in Pennsylvania. Horrific terrorist attacks had occurred prior to 9/11, such as the killing of 11 Israeli athletes and coaches at the 1972 Munich Olympics. However, the attack on 9/11 began a new era of terrorism because of its magnitude and the fact that it occurred on U.S. soil. As noted in the foreword of the 2002 report by the U.S. Joint Economic Committee entitled "Security in the Information Age," "the September 11 attacks on the World Trade Center and the Pentagon make it clear that we must be better aware of our vulnerabilities and develop viable strategies to detect, deter and counter both physical and cyber-based threats to our people and our infrastructure."[2]

Since 9/11, numerous other major terrorist attacks have occurred around the world, including the bombing of several trains in Madrid on March 11, 2004, the killing of hundreds of people in a Russian school on September 3, 2004, the bombings of London Underground trains and a bus on July 7, 2005, and the bombings in Sharm El-Sheik, Egypt, on July 23, 2005. Events such as these have changed the way in which the world views terrorism. In the United States, this change included passage of the Homeland Security Act of 2002,[3] establishing the U.S. Department of Homeland Security (DHS). The establishment of the DHS represents one of the largest changes in the organizational structure of the U.S. federal government in modern times.

The primary focus of the DHS was initially on protecting the homeland by improving physical security at such places as U.S. air-

---

[2] See Saxton (2002).

[3] For the full text, see Homeland Security Act of 2002 (2002).

ports and other border crossings. However, from its inception, this new cabinet-level department had an organizational subcomponent (with its own undersecretary) known as the Information Analysis and Infrastructure Protection Directorate. In June 2003, the National Cyber Security Division (NCSD) was created under this directorate to "identify, analyze, and reduce cyber threats and vulnerabilities; disseminate threat warning information; coordinate incident response; and provide technical assistance in continuity of operations and recovery planning."[4] The NCSD has served as the national focal point for cybersecurity issues for both the public and the private sectors. The NCSD activities were the direct responsibility of the Assistant Secretary for Infrastructure Protection. However, the growing importance of national cybersecurity activities has led the Secretary of DHS, Michael Chertoff, to create a new Assistant Secretary of Cyber and Telecommunications Security. This new position raises the visibility of cybersecurity activities at DHS.

In January 2004, the NCSD unveiled the National Cyber Alert System, an operational system designed to deliver timely and actionable information to the public regarding the security of their computer systems. The system is managed by the United States Computer Emergency Readiness Team (US-CERT), a partnership between the DHS and the private sector. The National Cyber Alert System "provides the first infrastructure for relaying graded computer security update and warning information to all users."[5] The program includes a series of information products distributed by e-mail targeting the needs of individuals, businesses, and government agencies.

The creation of a new Assistant Secretary of Cyber and Telecommunications Security is in line with the effort to implement President George W. Bush's National Strategy to Secure Cyberspace. As noted in the executive summary, the "National

---

[4] U.S. Department of Homeland Security (2003).

[5] U.S. Department of Homeland Security (2004).

Strategy to Secure Cyberspace is part of our overall effort to protect the Nation. It is an implementing component of the National Strategy for Homeland Security and is complemented by a National Strategy for the Physical Protection of Critical Infrastructures and Key Assets."[6,7]

The focus of the U.S. policy on cyberspace security is on three key strategic objectives. These objectives, which are consistent with the National Strategy for Homeland Security, are as follows:

• Prevent cyber attacks against America's critical infrastructures.

• Reduce national vulnerability to cyber attacks.

• Minimize damage and recovery time from cyber attacks that do occur.

Cybersecurity breaches affecting the *critical infrastructure assets* (the physical and cyberspace systems required to operate the economy and the government) of a country have the potential to have a significant impact on the national security of that country. Thus, the National Strategy to Secure Cyberspace issued by the White House in February 2003 cites cybersecurity as a key aspect of securing the nation's critical infrastructure.[8] As noted in this document, the critical U.S. infrastructures include public and private institutions in the following sectors: agriculture, food, water, public health, emergency services, government, defense industrial base, information and telecommunications, energy, transportation, banking and finance, chemicals and hazardous materials, and postal and shipping.

---

[6] U.S. Office of Homeland Security (2002), p. vii.

[7] For a full description of the National Strategy for the Protection of Critical Infrastructures and Key Assets, see White House (2003a).

[8] For a full description of the National Strategy to Secure Cyberspace, see White House (2003b).

The National Strategy to Secure Cyberspace articulates the following five national priorities:

1. A national cyberspace security response system
2. A national cyberspace security threat and vulnerability reduction program
3. A national cyberspace security awareness and training program
4. Securing governments' cyberspace
5. National security and international cyberspace security cooperation

These priorities can be thought of in terms of five levels, as depicted in Figure 8-1.

Since over 80 percent of the critical infrastructure assets of the United States are owned by firms in the private sector, it is not surprising that the U.S. National Strategy to Secure Cyberspace emphasizes the fact that the organizations within the private sector need to play a pivotal role in cyberspace security related to critical infrastructure assets. Thus, even at the national level, the importance of managing cybersecurity resources within private-sector organizations is critical. This point was highlighted in the resignation press conference of former DHS secretary Tom Ridge, as noted in Chapter 6.

Of course, managing cybersecurity resources within public-sector organizations effectively is also critical to successfully achieving the objectives of a rational strategy to secure cyberspace. In this latter regard, it is worth noting that a key mantra of government organizations is to take a business approach (make the business case) to resource allocation decisions.

These efforts notwithstanding, there are many who believe that the U.S. government has not properly addressed the cybersecurity threats and, more generally, the intelligence concerns confronting this country. As an outgrowth of these concerns, in December

FIGURE 8-1 Priorities in national strategy to secure cyberspace.

Priorities / Levels	Priorities and Level of Responsibilities in Securing Cyberspace				
	Priority 1 — National Cyberspace Security Response System	Priority 2 — National Cyberspace Security Threat and Vulnerability Reduction System	Priority 3 — National Cyberspace Security Awareness and Training Program	Priority 4 — Securing Government Cyberspace	Priority 5 — National Security and International Cyberspace Security Cooperation
Home user/ small business		X	X		
Large enterprises	X	X	X	X	X
Critical sectors/ infrastructures	X	X	X	X	X
National issues and vulnerabilities	X	X	X	X	
Global					X

Priority 1: Rapid responses in identification, information exchange, and remediation to mitigate the damage caused by malicious cyberspace activity.

Priority 2: To reduce threats and related vulnerabilities existing in current information assets, "National Strategy to Secure Cyberspace" identifies eight major actions and initiatives.

Priority 3: To increase the cybersecurity awareness and trained personnel in addressing cyber vulnerabilities, four major actions and initiatives for awareness, education, and training.

Priority 4: Securing government cyberspace is a priority because government performs at all essential levels of services and can lead as an example in cyberspace security in transactions with the private sector.

Priority 5: To better enable the United States to safeguard and defend its critical systems and networks, international cooperation can facilitate information sharing, reduce vulnerabilities, and deter malicious acts.

Source: White House, "National Strategy to Secure Cyberspace" (2003).

145

2004, President Bush signed the National Intelligence Reform Act of 2004. This law, which was a direct outgrowth of the 9/11 Commission Report,[9] seeks to reform the intelligence community and the intelligence and intelligence-related activities of the U.S. government. The National Intelligence Reform Act established the National Intelligence Authority as an independent agency within the executive branch of the U.S. government. This independent agency is headed by the national intelligence director. This act also amended the Clinger-Cohen Act, formerly known as the Information Technology Management Reform Act,[10] to include cybersecurity in systems planning by federal agencies.

According to the National Intelligence Reform Act, the key missions of the National Intelligence Authority are to (1) unify and strengthen the efforts of the intelligence community of the U.S. government, (2) ensure the organization of the efforts of the intelligence community of the U.S. government in a joint manner relating to intelligence missions rather than through intelligence collection disciplines, (3) provide for the operation of the National Counterterrorism Center and national intelligence centers, (4) eliminate barriers that impede coordination of the counterterrorism activities of the U.S. government between foreign intelligence activities located abroad and foreign intelligence activities located domestically while ensuring the protection of civil liberties, and (5) establish clear responsibility and accountability for counterterrorism and other intelligence matters relating to the national security of the United States.

The preceding discussion makes it clear that in a world that depends on computer-based information systems, cybersecurity is an

---

[9] For more information, see National Commission on Terrorist Attacks (2004).

[10] The focus of the Clinger-Cohen Act is on streamlining information technology acquisitions, including the purchase of commercial off-the-shelf systems, and emphasizing life-cycle management of IT as a capital investment. For more information, see Clinger-Cohen Act (1996).

essential element of national security. Indeed, as noted by the former secretary of the U.S. Department of Homeland Security, Tom Ridge, cybersecurity cuts across all aspects of a nation's critical infrastructure protection.[11] The critical importance of cybersecurity to national security has also been recognized by other industrialized countries.

Industrialized countries around the world now have government agencies that address cybersecurity issues in a manner similar to the way in which the U.S. government handles such issues. For example, in Japan, the Cabinet Secretariat's IT Security Office is responsible for developing and implementing countermeasures against cyber attacks and, in general, heads the country's efforts to coordinate all cybersecurity initiatives, including those related to partnerships between the public and private sectors.[12] In April 2004, Canada released its first comprehensive statement on national security, detailing in part its interests and strategy concerning cybersecurity issues. The creation of the Integrated Threat Assessment Centre, in cooperation with the establishment of a national Cybersecurity Task Force, was a direct result of Canada's need to address this key issue in its national security.[13] The European Union responded to the increased focus on cybersecurity with the creation of the European Network and Information Security Agency (ENISA). ENISA, which became effective in January 2004, is headquartered in Brussels, Belgium. Like several other newly emerging cross-national efforts developed to address issues of global cybersecurity, ENISA's main goal is to aid in the coordination of information security for its member nations.[14]

Figure 8-2 summarizes the national efforts related to cybersecurity discussed here, along with the efforts of several other nations.

[11] See White House (2003b).

[12] For more information, see U.S. Embassy in Tokyo, Japan (2003).

[13] See Office of the Prime Minister of Canada (2004).

[14] Leyden (2003).

FIGURE 8-2 Cybersecurity in selected countries.

Nation	Organization/Office	Major Responsibilities/Activities	Year Established	Supporting Body
Australia	National Security Division	Oversees all security agencies and national infrastructure initiatives; sets policy	2003	Attorney General's Department, Department of Defense, ASIS, Australian Federal Police
Canada	Integrated Threat Assessment Centre; Cyber Security Task Force	Produces comprehensive integrated threat assessments relating to the security of Canada; brings together threat-related information for assessment and deployment	2004	Department of Public Safety and Emergency Preparedness
China	Bureau of Public Information and Internet Security Supervision	Combats Internet-based financial crimes, information warfare, and terrorist activities; protects public and private software and hardware facilities; monitors online content; prepares for cyber-based emergencies		Ministry of Public Security, China Computer Federation, Ministry of National Security
European Union	ENISA (European Network and Information Security)	Aids in the coordination of information security for member nations	2004	

Germany	BSI (Federal Office for Information Security)	Operates as central IT security service provider for the German government; investigates security risks and develops preventive security measures; provides information on risks and threats; responsible for testing and assessment of IT systems; analyzes developments and trends in information technology	1990	German Federal Ministry of the Interior
India	Department of Information Technology	Coordinates all cybersecurity initiatives		Ministry of Communications and Information Technology
Japan	Cabinet Secretariat's IT Security Office	Develops and implements countermeasures against cyberattacks; heads efforts in coordinating all cyber security initiatives including those related to e-government and initiatives, involving private-sector partnerships		
Russia	FSB (Federal Security Service) Computer and Information Security Directorate	Coordinates activities of all agencies involved in information security protection; counterintelligence activity and the fight against crime in the sphere of computer and information security	1998	Federal Agency of Government Communications and Information (FAPSI)

(*Continued on next page.*)

FIGURE 8-2 (*Continued*)

Nation	Organization / Office	Major Responsibilities / Activities	Year Established	Supporting Body
South Korea	NCSC (National Cyber Security Centre)	Coordinates all cybersecurity initiatives		Defense Ministry, National Police Agency, Information Ministry
Spain	CSI (Consejo Superior de Informática)	Prepares, develops, and enforces government policy on computer systems; the Technical Committee on the Security of Information Systems and Personal Data Processing (subcommittee SSITAD) unifies information systems and security-related actions among all government departments, defines common policies and procedures, provides training, fosters general awareness		Ministry of Public Administration; Guardia Civil; Policía Nacional

Country	Agency	Description	Year	Reporting to
Switzerland	CYCO (Swiss Coordination Unit for Cybercrime Control)	Coordinates the fight against Internet crime at the federal level; acts as a countrywide center for reporting suspicious events; conducts investigations into illegal content on the Internet; analyzes criminal incidents on the Internet	2003	Swiss Federal Strategic Unit for Information Technology (FSUIT), Permanent Analysis and Reporting Centre for Information Security (MELANI), Task Force on Information Assurance (SONIA)
United States	National Cyber Security Division (NCSD)	Identifies, analyzes, and reduces cyber threats and vulnerabilities; disseminates threat warning information; coordinates incident response; and provides technical assistance in continuity of operations and recovery planning	2003	Department of Homeland Security

This table is intended to be suggestive, rather than all-inclusive, of the type of national cybersecurity efforts that are under way.

Local governments have also been engaged in improving cybersecurity. In the United States, every state has an ongoing, active cybersecurity program. Efforts at the state level have also resulted in a myriad of legislative actions, with California, Michigan, New York, and Utah being among the leaders in this regard.[15]

Corporate disclosure of cybersecurity activities

In her thought-provoking editorial, the editor-in-chief of *Information Week* put forth the following dare: "Are you confident enough in your processes, policies, and technologies to say that customer data is safe? Are you confident enough to put it in your annual report? Are you confident enough to guarantee it to all of your customers?"[16]

How much information should a corporation voluntarily disclose about its cybersecurity activities (including actual breaches and the size and composition of its computer security expenditures) to interested parties such as employees, business partners, customers, creditors, investors, government agencies, and the general public? Clearly, compliance with government regulations and legislation must be considered in addressing this question. However, it is instructive to first address the question without considering government regulations and in the context of corporate disclosure within the private sector of an economy.

One would expect that disclosure of a corporation's information security activity would affect the organization's strategic position in the marketplace. If a firm were to disclose information concern-

---

[15] For one overview of state cybersecurity programs, see Computer Security Industry Alliance (2004).

[16] See Stahl (2005), p. 6.

ing actual security breaches, it might well suffer a loss of competitive advantage. In other words, given the empirical results discussed in Chapter 3, it seems fair to expect that some customers and suppliers would choose to sever their ties with a firm that reported breaches involving compromising confidential information.

Suppose the corporation were to disclose information about its cybersecurity expenditures, but not reveal information about actual breaches that have occurred. Such a disclosure might have countervailing effects. For example, if a firm reveals that it has an active and impressive cybersecurity program, it may gain market share, attracting customers by giving them increased comfort and confidence in dealing with the firm. To the extent that this is true, one would expect firms to voluntarily reveal such cybersecurity information. Additionally, economically rational computer hackers seeking (illegal) bounty would shy away from devoting their resources to attacking systems where the probability of a successful attack has been lowered and the cost of a successful attack has been raised.[17] Of course, the reverse situation would also hold. That is, a firm that reveals that its cybersecurity programs are weak would be likely to invite more, rather than fewer, hackers to attack their systems.

However, if some hackers enjoy the challenge of penetrating the most protected systems (and there is anecdotal evidence to support this contention), reporting a high level of information security activity could actually make the firm a target for security breaches. Moreover, some consumers, vendors, and potential business partners might interpret the organization's active security program as a signal that the organization has severe cybersecurity problems, leading these parties to withdraw from interacting with the organization.

[17] Schechter and Smith (2003) develop a formal economic model to make this point.

In sum, we can see that corporations face contradictory incentives in determining the degree to which they should voluntarily disclose their cybersecurity activities. However, the freedom of corporations to determine their degree of cybersecurity disclosure is constrained by mandatory disclosure legislation and regulations. In response to the many accounting scandals involving U.S. corporations that began to surface in the late 1990s, the U.S. Congress passed, and President Bush signed into law, the Sarbanes-Oxley Act of 2002. This complex law dramatically affects corporate governance and financial disclosure for publicly traded U.S. corporations and for corporations from other countries that wish to be listed on U.S. stock exchanges. Section 302 of the act requires the chief executive officer and the chief financial officer of a corporation to take personal responsibility for the establishment and maintenance of the firm's internal controls and to certify that the firm's financial statements fairly represent the company's financial condition. Title IV of the act, "Enhanced Financial Disclosures," is germane to the issue of cybersecurity disclosures. Of particular relevance is Section 404, which requires corporations to include an internal control report in their annual reports. The internal control report must

> (1) state the responsibility of management for establishing and maintaining an adequate internal control structure and procedures for financial reporting; and (2) contain an assessment, as of the end of the most recent fiscal year of the issuer, of the effectiveness of the internal control structure and procedures of the issuer for financial reporting.[18]

Furthermore, the firm's external auditor must "attest to, and report on" management's assessment of the internal control system.

Section 404 of the Sarbanes-Oxley Act required the U.S. Securities and Exchange Commission (SEC) to prescribe rules guiding

[18] For the full text, see Sarbanes-Oxley Act (2002).

the internal control report. The SEC has released such guidelines, and for a small set of firms, compliance with the new internal control report began with annual reports covering fiscal years ending on or after June 15, 2004 (for most firms, however, compliance did not begin until April 15, 2005).[19,20]

The SEC clearly notes that a major portion of a firm's internal control structure is focused on safeguarding the company's assets (including its information assets) and ensuring that the data used for financial reporting and internal decision making are accurate and reliable. In a contemporary computer-based environment, we believe that any meaningful report on the firm's internal control system, such as that required under Section 404 of the Sarbanes-Oxley Act, should include a discussion of the firm's information and system security activities. Our view is consistent with that expressed by the Cyber Security Industry Alliance when it noted, "Review of these statutory and administrative materials clearly indicates that compliance with Section 404 Sox requires publicly traded companies to employ information security to the extent necessary to ensure the effectiveness of internal controls over financial reporting."[21] The Sarbanes-Oxley Act gives organizations a tremendous incentive to allocate substantially more resources to cybersecurity activities than heretofore has been the case. In fact, any move toward more disclosure of cybersecurity activities, whether voluntary or involuntary in nature, should result in resources being shifted from other organizational activities to cybersecurity activities. Of course, the larger the amount of resources spent on cybersecurity activities, the more important is the effective management of such resources.

[19] See U.S. Securities and Exchange Commission (2003).

[20] For an interesting article discussing the impact of the Sarbanes-Oxley Act on the role of the CIO versus the CFO, see Koch (2004).

[21] Cyber Security Industry Alliance "Sarbanes-Oxley Act: Implementation of Information Technology and Security Objectives," (2004) p. 2.

In addition to the Sarbanes-Oxley Act, there are other laws and legislative proposals that currently or potentially affect cybersecurity disclosure, and in turn resource allocation decisions, in the United States. The recent California Security Breach Information Act (S.B. 1386), which requires notification of confidentiality breaches, is one example. This act requires any agency or organization that experiences a data security breach to inform "any resident of California whose unencrypted personal information was, or is reasonably believed to have been, acquired by an unauthorized person."[22] In 2003, Congressman Adam Putnam, the chairman of the House Government Reform Subcommittee on Technology, Information Policy, Intergovernmental Relations and the Census, proposed the Corporate Information Security Accountability Act of 2003.[23] Although this legislation was not enacted, it is always possible that similar legislation mandating cybersecurity disclosure could pass in the future.

Since a large percentage of the critical infrastructure assets of the United States is owned by firms in the private sector, disclosure of corporate cybersecurity activities also has the potential for significantly affecting national security. Accordingly, any government regulation aimed at increasing corporate disclosure needs to consider the national security implications. For example, if firms in the energy, telecommunications, and financial industries are required to report all of their security breaches or investments in security activities, how much more vulnerable does it make these industries to cyber attacks? In other words, the trade-off between the public's need to have access to more information and the need to maintain national security via privacy of information is ever-present.

---

[22] For the full text of this act, see California Security Breach Information Act (2002).

[23] For the full text of this proposed legislation, see Corporate Information Security Accountability Act (2003).

Government disclosure of cybersecurity activities

Government organizations face many of the same issues that corporations confront when it comes to disclosure of cybersecurity activities. For example, disclosure of weaknesses in cybersecurity programs is likely to invite more hackers in search of easy targets. In contrast, disclosure of strong cybersecurity programs may dissuade hackers from attacking the information systems of a particular government agency.

In the U.S. federal government, agencies with inspector generals are evaluated each year on their information security activities, as mandated by the Federal Information Security Management Act (FISMA) of 2002. These evaluations are publicly disclosed in a report card–style summary. The report card grades for 24 federal government agencies for the years 2002 to 2004 are provided in Figure 8-3. As indicated in Figure 8-3, seven agencies, including the Department of Homeland Security, received a failing grade for 2004. In addition, five other agencies received a D grade for 2004. Only two agencies, the Agency for International Development and the Department of Transportation, received an A grade. Despite the dismal nature of these grades for 2004, a quick look at Figure 8-3 reveals the fact that the trend over the past three years is positive. The grades shown in Figure 8-3 are based on agency reports filed in compliance with FISMA.

The poor computer security grades in the U.S. federal government have led to the formation of the CISO (Chief Information Security Officer) Exchange.[24] The objective of the CISO Exchange is to improve IT security in the federal government through an exchange of information between the public and private sectors. The CISO Exchange's activities include, but are not limited to, meetings,

---

[24] See Government Technology (2005).

FIGURE 8-3   Federal computer security grades, 2002–2004[a,b].

Government-wide Grade 2004: D+

	2004	2003	2002
Agency for International Development*	A+	C-	F
Department of Transportation	A-	D+	F
Nuclear Regulatory Commission	B+	A	C
Social Security Administration	B	B+	B-
Environmental Protection Agency	B	C	D-
Department of Labor	B-	B	C+
Department of Justice	B-	F	F
General Services Administration	C+	D	D
National Science Foundation	C+	A-	D-
Department of the Interior	C+	F	F
Department of Education	C	C+	D
Office of Personnel Management	C-	D-	F
Department of State	D+	F	F
Department of the Treasury**	D+	D	F
Department of Defense**	D	D	F
National Aeronautics and Space Administration	D-	D-	D+
Small Business Administration	D-	C-	F
Department of Commerce	F	C-	D+
Department of Veterans Affairs**	F	C	F
Department of Agriculture	F	F	F
Department of Health and Human Services	F	F	D-
Department of Energy	F	F	F
Department of Housing and Urban Development	F	F	F
Department of Homeland Security	F	F	—

* Inspector General did not submit an independent evaluation of the agency's security management program as required by the Federal Information Security Management Act of 2002.

** No independent evaluation from the Inspector General was submitted in 2003.

[a] "2004 Federal Computer Security Report Card" is based on reports required by the Federal Information Security Management Act of 2002. See Subcommittee on Technology, Information Policy Intergovernmental Relations and the Census (2004).

[b] "2003 Federal Computer Security Report Card" is based on reports required by the Federal Information Security Management Act of 2002. See Subcommittee on Technology, Information Policy Intergovernmental Relations and the Census (2003).

exchanging best practices, and the production of an annual report covering IT security and operational issues.

Of course, mandatory public disclosure of the effectiveness, or more specifically the ineffectiveness, of information security activities within U.S. federal government agencies raises an interesting national security dilemma. That is, mandatory public disclosure provides U.S. citizens with transparency in terms of the way information security resources are being managed within federal government agencies. It also provides a strong career-related incentive for agency managers to correct their security weaknesses. In this latter regard, although we do not know the specific repercussions of agencies getting low grades, presumably such low grades will negatively affect the careers of the managers responsible for computer security. Everything else held constant, both of these outcomes should lead to a more efficient allocation of cybersecurity resources. However, everything else is not held constant because publicly disclosing the security weaknesses of various government agencies sends up a red flare to hackers that such systems are vulnerable to attack. As a result, more hacking is likely to take place, and more cybersecurity resources will be required to offset the threat of cybersecurity breaches. Given the generally espoused U.S. philosophy of "more transparency is preferred to less," federal government agencies may err on the side of too much disclosure, rather than too little, when it comes to cybersecurity activities. Of course, this tendency is being tempered by the concern for national security, especially since 9/11.

Externalities and information sharing

As discussed in the first chapter of this book, the inherent interconnectivity of computer networks creates what economists call network externalities (i.e., spillover effects) that are not easily addressed by normal market mechanisms. When customers, vendors, and international trade partners are connected to a computer network (e.g., the Internet), some benefits (positive externalities) automatically spill over to all those who are connected to the same network. Similarly, when individuals and organizations connect to a computer network with the intention of committing theft or vandalism, negative externalities accrue to other network users. Additional externalities arise because the security of the network depends on the cybersecurity activities of each user of the network. Hence, a benign but careless user of the network (e.g., a user that does not install antivirus software) reduces the security of all network users.

Since the security of a computer network depends on the actions taken by all users of the network, it is not surprising that significant efforts are underway to coordinate cybersecurity activities on both a national and an international level. One form of such cooperation is the notion of "information sharing" on issues of importance concerning cybersecurity. Several organizations have been formed over the years to foster such information-sharing arrangements. In the United States, US-CERT, INFRAGARD, the Center for Internet Security, and the Information Sharing and Analysis Centers (ISACs) are all involved in facilitating information sharing on issues related to cybersecurity.[25] These organizations hope to increase overall cybersecurity by having their members share information in a timely manner on how best to prevent computer security breaches and on threats and actual attacks that

---

[25] INFRAGARD is a cooperative undertaking among business, academic institutions, and all levels of government with the purpose of increasing the security of the United States's critical infrastructures. For more information, see http://www.infragard.net/. For specific details on ISACs, the reader is referred to http://www.ni2ciel.org/ISACs.

members experience. The U.S. government played a key role in the creation of the most prominent information-sharing organizations and, through the Department of Homeland Security, continues to take an active interest in promoting the efficient operations of these organizations. For example, Presidential Decision Directive/NSC-63 (PDD-63), Critical Infrastructure Protection, dated May 22, 1998, set in motion the creation of ISACs.

From the point of view of an individual organization or country, information sharing holds the promise of providing increased security at a lower cost. That is, information sharing provides a mechanism for managing cybersecurity resources more efficiently. Consider a simple computer network shared by 10 organizations. Suppose that without sharing, each organization spends $10,000 on information security. Because of the externalities, the funds spent on cybersecurity activities by one organization will benefit, at least to some extent, all nine other organizations sharing the computer network. Now suppose all firms fully share information about (1) their methods for preventing breaches, (2) their methods for reducing their losses should a breach occur, and (3) the actual intrusions and breaches that they experience. Assuming that this information sharing takes place, more of the benefits from the cybersecurity spending of all of the organizations on the network will spill over. Thus, each organization may get the same level of security by spending $10,000 with sharing as it would have gotten by spending $14,000 without sharing. In other words, if each firm shares the information described and maintains information security expenditures at the $10,000 level, each firm will have increased security (face a lower probability of an information security breach) at no extra cost. Alternatively, each firm involved in the sharing arrangement could react to sharing by lowering its information security expenditure level while still achieving the same or a higher level of protection from cyber attacks.[26]

Although information sharing holds the promise of increased security at a reduced cost, companies and nations are generally concerned about the costs associated with sharing. These costs go well beyond the direct costs of gathering information and sharing it with other members of an information-sharing organization. Indeed, the costs go to the heart of strategic organizational and national concerns. For example, suppose a member company that belongs to an information-sharing organization believes that the anonymity of the supplier of information cannot be guaranteed. In this case, the company probably would not share freely, fearing that information it revealed about a security breach would become available to competitors and be used to steal its customers.

Even if a company believes that anonymity will be guaranteed, it is likely that the company would not fully share security information. Since the benefits from a company's sharing information about security activities are derived by other members of the sharing group, withholding information has no direct effect on the benefits to the company sharing the information. However, withholding information does affect the benefits derived by the other members of the sharing group. To the extent that the other members of the sharing group are competitors in the marketplace, each individual company would gain some competitive advantage by withholding information. This type of analysis often leads members of an information-sharing group to a situation where they provide a little information about their activities in the hope of

[26] This discussion on information sharing is largely based on Gordon, Loeb, and Lucyshyn (2003b). This article presents a rigorous economic model and analysis of information sharing. Using that model, the authors show that each organization always spends no more (and often less) on security with sharing than without sharing. See Krishnan, Smith, and Telang (2003) and Schechter and Smith (2003) for additional analyses of other aspects of information sharing.

learning a lot about the activities of the other members of the information-sharing group. This type of behavior is referred to as the *free-rider problem*, and it works against information-sharing organizations reaching their full potential.

Given this discussion, it becomes apparent that the ideal benefits from information-sharing arrangements can be achieved only if the appropriate economic incentives required to prevent (or at least minimize) free-riding behavior are in place. Unfortunately, these incentives are currently not in place in connection with the existing information-sharing arrangements related to cybersecurity.

Implications

The security of a nation is, in part, dependent on cybersecurity. Thus, there should be little surprise in the fact that centralized government organizations in industrialized countries are spending significant amounts of money on cybersecurity activities. Nowhere is the trend toward spending significant amounts on cybersecurity activities more prevalent than within the U.S. federal government.

As more resources are devoted to cybersecurity activities, the need to manage such resources efficiently becomes all the more important. This point is especially true when one considers the interaction between cybersecurity activities and national security. That is, the security of a nation is clearly affected by the way cybersecurity resources are managed. Thought of in these terms, managing cybersecurity resources efficiently translates into the most important goal confronting a civilized society—protecting human lives.

The effective management of these resources should be based on the principle of cost-benefit analysis discussed in the earlier chapters of this book. In other words, effective management of cybersecurity resources by public-sector organizations should parallel the management of such resources within private-sector organizations. The one big difference, of course, is that once you bring in the consideration of national security, quantifying the benefits of cybersecurity activities becomes a far more difficult task than it is when such a concern is not present. This difficulty notwithstanding, it is still imperative to compare the benefits of cybersecurity activities to their costs.

One way to potentially increase the efficiency of the resources allocated to cybersecurity is for organizations and nations to share information related to cybersecurity activities. Consequently, it is no surprise that many such sharing arrangements have surfaced over the past decade. Unfortunately, because of the free-rider problem, *it is a myth to assume that existing efforts directed toward information sharing have significantly reduced cybersecurity-related problems or will do so in the future. The reality is that for information sharing to be effective in the cybersecurity arena, the appropriate economic incentives will first have to be put in place.* Deriving the appropriate economic incentives is a fertile area for research, and several individuals are taking up this challenge.

9

CONCLUDING COMMENTS

It is tough to make predictions, especially about the future.

—YOGI BERRA (AMERICAN BASEBALL PLAYER)

HE INTERNET IS one of the greatest innovations of the twentieth century. Undeniably, the Internet has changed the daily lives of millions of individuals and thousands of organizations around the world. There is no longer any doubt that we live in an information-based environment that transcends national borders. This information-based environment has opened the doors to many wonderful global opportunities for individuals and organizations alike.

However, new problems generally accompany major innovations.[1] This is certainly true of the advent of the Internet. One of these problems, although not the focus of this book, is the fact that there is so much information readily available that "information overload" is a prevalent concern for many people and organizations. Information search and filtering rules, as well as methods for analyzing large sets of information, are ways of addressing this concern.[2]

Cybersecurity is another problem associated with the Internet. As noted in the first chapter, cybersecurity is concerned with protecting information that is accessed and transmitted via the Internet. A basic argument embedded throughout this book is that technical security solutions (e.g., access controls, firewalls, and intrusion detection systems) for improving cybersecurity are necessary, but not sufficient, for minimizing the cybersecurity problem. That is, cybersecurity is as much about management (making sound business decisions) as it is about finding technical solutions. The more specific argument carried throughout this book is that managing cybersecurity resources efficiently is also necessary, although not sufficient, for minimizing the problems associated with the lack of information security. Thus, the primary objective of this book has been to present a cost-benefit framework for managing an organization's cybersecurity resources efficiently. This framework is applicable to organizations within both the private and public sectors of an economy.

Spend wisely and reap the benefits

Organizations have finite resources to allocate to a large number of competing needs. These needs include, but are not limited to,

[1] Another of mankind's greatest innovations is the automobile. However, automobile accidents are a major cause of death in most industrialized countries.

[2] The need to analyze and understand large sets of information (data) has created a new area of study called data mining.

production, marketing, accounting, finance, information technology, and personnel activities. All of these activities depend on information, and the security of that information. Thus, organizational resources need to be allocated to cybersecurity activities as a means of assuring that the other functions of the organization can be carried out successfully. More to the point, the managers in charge of cybersecurity need to be able to make the business case for their fair share of organizational resources. This book has provided these managers with the financial tools, and an understanding of how to apply these tools, necessary to make the business case for obtaining an adequate level of funding for cybersecurity activities.

The benefits of cybersecurity activities are derived from the cost savings associated with preventing breaches. Organizations that spend wisely, weighing the costs of protecting the confidentiality, integrity, and availability of their information systems against the expected costs of information security breaches, are in a position to reap substantial benefits. In contrast, organizations that do not spend wisely on cybersecurity either are exposing themselves to unnecessary risks of information breaches and resulting losses or are unnecessarily draining funds that could be used elsewhere in the organization to foster increased efficiency and growth.

Wireless security

A growing trend among organizations in both the private and public sectors of an economy is the rapid movement toward wireless communication. This trend is due to the fact that wireless communications tend to provide more flexibility and, as a result, increase user efficiency. At the same time, the costs of such systems are often much lower than the costs of wired systems because of the elimination of some wiring costs. However, wireless communication systems also pose additional security concerns related to the confidentiality, integrity, and availability of information because the medium of communication, the airwaves, is more vulnerable to intruders than is normally the case with totally wired systems.

The management of resources related to the security of wireless communication systems needs to be based on the principle of cost-benefit analysis, similar to that discussed throughout this book. Now, however, an added dimension to consider is whether it pays to go wireless or to remain wired. In its discussions of wireless network security within U.S. federal government agencies, NIST noted, "Agencies should be aware that maintaining a secure wireless network is an ongoing process that requires greater effort than that required for other networks and systems. Moreover, it is important that agencies assess risks more frequently and test and evaluate system security controls when wireless technologies are deployed."[3] In other words, there is an economic trade-off between going wireless and staying wired, as well as a cost-benefit issue related to different wireless options. Once again, NIST hit the proverbial nail on the head when it noted, "Agencies should perform a risk assessment and develop a security policy before purchasing wireless technologies, because their unique security requirements will determine which products should be considered for purchase."[4] Of course, as discussed in Chapter 5, risk management is itself an illusory concept in the context of cybersecurity.

Cybersecurity realities

In the first chapter, we outlined five myths about cybersecurity that many people believe to be true. As we have explored various topics surrounding cybersecurity, we have uncovered the realities

[3] Karygiannis and Owens (2002).

[4] Ibid.

of cybersecurity. The aforementioned myths can now be restated as the following five cybersecurity realities:

Reality 1: Cost-benefit analysis can and should be applied to cybersecurity activities.

Reality 2: A large portion of cybersecurity breaches does not have a significant economic impact on organizations. However, the cybersecurity breaches associated with confidentiality do indeed tend to have a significant economic impact on organizations.

Reality 3: Cybersecurity investments can and should be determined in a rational economic manner.

Reality 4: The full scope of risk management related to cybersecurity is inadequately understood by many cybersecurity managers.

Reality 5: For information sharing to be effective in the cybersecurity arena, the appropriate economic incentives must be put in place.

Historical perspective on cybersecurity in the United States

Cybersecurity is an issue of concern that is a direct outgrowth of the Internet. Thus, the term *cybersecurity* is one that emerged during the 1990s. This fact notwithstanding, concern for the security of computer-based information predates the development of the Internet by several decades. In the United States, for example, the U.S. Department of Defense (DoD) established standards for evaluating the security of computer systems (relating to both hardware and software) back in 1985. DoD's standards, which became known as "the Orange Book," represent the minimum threshold for vendors wishing to sell DoD computer systems. It is generally believed that the Orange Book was instrumental in pushing the computer industry toward building more secure computer systems. Many of the security gains achieved because of the Orange Book (e.g., those related to access control), have laid the groundwork for modern cybersecurity activities.

The standards perpetuated under the Orange Book were geared toward the handling of "classified" or "sensitive" information utilized by the U.S. federal government. At the time, the U.S. federal government accounted for a large portion of the demand for secure computer systems. By the late 1980s, it became obvious that the security required for classified or sensitive information was far more stringent than that required for nonsensitive information. The Computer Security Act of 1987 relaxed the federal government's need to utilize Orange Book–type secure systems by limiting this requirement to systems that handled sensitive information.

By the early 1990s, the commercial and personal demand for computers was in full swing. This fact, coupled with the relaxation of standards for federal government computer systems that did not handle classified or sensitive information, gave computer manufacturers an incentive to turn their efforts more toward producing efficient computers and away, at least in part, from producing secure systems. The Clinger-Cohen Act of 1996, which encouraged federal government agencies to purchase commercial off-the-shelf computer systems whenever possible, provided an even greater incentive for computer manufacturers to deemphasize computer security.

By the mid- to late 1990s, the world was engulfed in the Internet revolution and the term *cybersecurity* became a household word. Concern for cybersecurity in the United States reached its peak after the 9/11 terrorist attacks. Indeed, since 9/11, there have been a large number of laws and initiatives within the United States that directly or indirectly affect cybersecurity. These laws and initiatives include the Department of Homeland Security Act of 2002, the National Intelligence Reform Act of 2004, the formation of the Cyber Security Industry Alliance in 2004, the CISO Exchange in 2005, and the publication of a report by the Commission on the Intelligence Capabilities of the United States Regarding Weapons of Mass Destruction in 2005. Figure 9-1 illustrates the key laws and initiatives that have played an important role in the development of cybersecurity within the United States that have been discussed throughout this book.

Future direction

In closing, it is important to emphasize that cybersecurity is a relatively new phenomenon confronting organizations and people around the world. Indeed, the full power and dangers of the Internet are only starting to be identified. However, when it comes to the Internet, Yogi Berra's claim that "it is tough to make predictions, especially about the future" certainly rings true. Nevertheless, one thing that does seem clear is that the future will not produce a "silver bullet" that will completely solve the problems related to cybersecurity. In fact, as one problem gets solved, a new one seems to emerge. In terms of new problems, one of the latest concerns is that of spyware. As the name suggests, *spyware* is software that embeds itself in a user's computer and monitors (i.e., spies on) the use of the computer without the user's knowledge or consent.

As long as scarce resources have to be allocated among competing needs, cost-benefit analysis can and should play an important role in managing an organization's cybersecurity. This is true whether the communication system is wired, wireless, or some combination thereof. Recent empirical evidence shows that many organizations have begun to realize this interconnectivity between cost-benefit analysis and cybersecurity. As difficult as it is to predict the future, we believe that this trend will continue.

FIGURE 9-1 Timeline of U.S. cybersecurity laws and initiatives.

1996	1998	1999	2001	2002	2003	2004	2005
• Clinger-Cohen Act • Health Insurance Portability and Accountability Act • "An Introduction to Computer Security: The NIST Handbook" published	• Presidential Decision Directive 63	• Graham-Leach-Bliley Act	• 9/11 Terrorist Attacks	• California Security Breach Information Act • Homeland Security Act • Sarbanes-Oxley Act • National Strategy for Homeland Security issued • Federal Information Security Management Act published	• National Strategy to Secure Cyberspace issued • National Strategy for the Protection of Critical Infrastructures and Key Asset issued • National Cyber Security Division created	• National Cyber Alert System unveiled • National Intelligence Reform Act	• CISO Exchange formed • Report by the Commission on the Intelligence Capabilities of the United States Regarding Weapons of Mass Destruction published

GLOSSARY

Agency theory   A framework for considering the way principals contract with agents to make decisions on their behalf.

Annual loss expectancy (ALE)   An approach that measures information security risk in terms of the annual loss expected with an information security investment.

Asymmetric information   A situation in which not everyone has the same information (e.g., managers have information that is not available to stockholders).

Authentication   Making sure that authorized users are who they claim to be.

Availability   Having information accessible by authorized users on a timely basis.

Capital investments   Expenditures that benefit operations for several periods. Also referred to as *capital expenditures*.

Certainty equivalent   The certain amount that leaves the decision maker indifferent between the certain amount and the risky return. For a risk-neutral manager, the certainty equivalent is the expected return on the investment.

Confidentiality   Protection of private information from *nonauthorized* users.

Cost-benefit analysis   Comparing the costs of an activity to the benefits from that activity, focusing on allocating resources efficiently among competing activities.

Cost of capital   The minimum rate that a project needs to earn if the organization's value is not to be reduced (i.e., the opportunity cost of funds).

Critical infrastructure assets   Physical and cyberspace systems that are required to operate an economy and a government.

Cybersecurity   Protection of information that is accessed and transmitted via the Internet or any other computer network. For purposes of this book, the terms *cybersecurity, computer security,* and *information security* are used interchangeably.

Cybersecurity auditing   A feedback control (monitoring) process for assessing existing security flaws.

Defense in depth   Having multiple layers of protection, such as restricting physical access to computers to authorized personnel and requiring passwords for operation.

Deferment option   The ability to postpone an investment.

Direct costs of cybersecurity breaches   Costs that can be clearly linked to specific breaches.

Encryption   The practice of encoding and decoding messages.

Enterprise risk management (ERM)   Overall process of managing an organization's exposure to uncertainty with particular emphasis on identifying and managing the events that could potentially prevent the organization from achieving its objectives.

Explicit costs of cybersecurity breaches   Fully revealed costs of cybersecurity breaches that can be measured in an unambiguous manner.

Firewall systems   Software and/or hardware used to prevent unauthorized access to or from private networks.

Free-rider problem   The situation in which members of a group provide only a little information about their activities but hope to learn a lot about the other members of the group.

GLEIS model   A rigorous mathematical approach to deriving the right amount to invest in cybersecurity activities, based on security breach functions.

Hacker   An individual who gains unauthorized access to a computer system.

Implicit costs of cybersecurity breaches   Costs of cybersecurity breaches that are not fully revealed (i.e., costs associated with lost opportunities).

Indirect costs of cybersecurity breaches   Costs that cannot be clearly linked to specific breaches.

Integrity   The accuracy, reliability, and validity of information.

Internal rate of return (IRR)   The discount rate that equates the present value of future cash inflows from a project to the project's initial cost. The IRR is also used as a method for selecting capital investments.

Internet   An electronic communications network that connects computers from around the world.

Intrusion detection system (IDS)   A system designed to detect security breaches after they have occurred.

Intrusion prevention system (IPS)   A system designed to prevent breaches by detecting unusual network traffic coming into the system.

Making the business case   The process whereby a proposal is prepared to justify the use of organizational resources in a particular manner rather than other possible alternative uses of those resources.

Management   Planning, directing, coordinating, and controlling the use of resources to accomplish a given objective.

National security   Protection of the security of a nation.

Net present value (NPV)   A method for selecting capital investments based on the difference between the present value of future cash inflows from a project and the project's initial cost.

Network externalities   Spillovers in benefits and costs to a user of the network resulting from the fact that many others are using the same network.

Nonrepudiation   Making sure that authorized users cannot deny the fact that they are the actual users.

Operating costs   Expenditures that benefit a single period's operations.

Opportunity costs   Costs associated with lost opportunities.

Penetration testing   Hacking one's own computer network.

Present value (PV)   The amount one is willing to pay today in exchange for the receipt of cash flows in the future.

Return on investment (ROI)   An accounting concept that is derived by dividing the annual profits (determined using accounting revenues and costs) by the cost of the investment.

Risk　The uncertainty of a potentially harmful event occurring.

Risk-averse　The attitude toward risk in which one prefers an investment with a certain return to one with an uncertain return with the same expected value.

Risk management　The process of identifying, controlling, and managing the impact of uncertain events (NIST, 1995, p. 59).

Risk-neutral　The attitude toward risk in which one is concerned only with the expected return on an investment.

Security incident　An event that compromises security.

Spyware　Software that embeds itself in a user's computer and monitors the use of the computer without the user's knowledge or consent.

Strategic option　The value associated with an investment today that properly positions the firm for the future.

Threats　The sources of potential actions or events that could cause information security breaches.

Virus　A malicious computer program that causes malfunctions in a computer system.

Vulnerabilities　Weaknesses in a computer information system that make attacks on the system likely to be successful.

ACRONYMS

AAA	American Accounting Association
ACM	Association for Computing Machinery
AHP	Analytical hierarchy process
ALE	Annual loss expectancy
B2B	Business-to-business
B2C	Business-to-consumer
B2G	Business-to-government
CEO	Chief executive officer
CERT	CERT Coordination Center
CFO	Chief financial officer
CIO	Chief information officer
CIS	Center for Internet Security
CISO	Chief information security officer
CISSP	Certified Information Systems Security Professional
CSI	Computer Security Institute

CSIA	Cyber Security Industry Alliance
CO	Cybersecurity officer
CSO	Chief security officer
DHS	Department of Homeland Security
ENISA	European Network and Information Security Agency
ERM	Enterprise risk management
FBI	Federal Bureau of Investigation
FIPS	Federal Information Processing Standard
FISMA	Federal Information Security Management Act
GAAP	Generally accepted accounting principles
GAISP	Generally accepted information security principles
GAO	Government Accountability Office (formerly called the General Accounting Office)
GASSP	Generally accepted system security principles
GLBA	Gramm-Leach-Bliley Act of 1999
HIPAA	Health Insurance Portability and Accountability Act of 1996
ICC	International Chamber of Commerce
ICSA	International Computer Security Association
IDS	Intrusion detection system
IEC	International Electrotechnical Commission
IEEE	Institute of Electrical and Electronics Engineers
IIA	Institute of Internal Auditors
IMA	Institute of Management Accountants
IPS	Intrusion prevention system
IRR	Internal rate of return
ISAC	Information Sharing and Analysis Center
ISACA	Information Systems Audit and Control Association

ISC²	International Information Systems Security Certifications Consortium, Inc.
ISO	International Organization for Standardization
ISSA	Information Systems Security Association
IT	Information technology
NCSD	National Cyber Security Division
NIST	National Institute of Standards and Technology
NPV	Net present value
NSA	National Security Agency
OECD	Organization for Economic Co-operation and Development
PV	Present value
ROI	Return on investment
ROSI	Return on security investment
SEC	Securities and Exchange Commission
SSCP	System Security Certified Practitioner
UN	United Nations
US-CERT	United States Computer Emergency Readiness Team

REFERENCES

Anderson, R.: "Why Information Security Is Hard—An Economic Perspective," *Proceedings of the 17th Annual Computer Security Applications Conference*, December 2001.

Asquiti, A.: "Privacy and Security of Personal Information: Economic Incentives and Technological Solutions," chapter 14 in L. Camp and S. Lewis (eds.), *Economics of Information Security*. Boston, MA.: Springer, 2004.

Bagchi, K., and G. Udo: "An Analysis of the Growth of Computer and Internet Security Breaches." *Communications of the Association for Information Systems*, vol. 12, December 2003, pp. 680–700.

Bank, D.: "Tighter Cyber Protection Is Urged by Computer-Security Industry," *Wall Street Journal,* Dec. 7, 2004, pp. A3, A10.

Bodin, L., L. A. Gordon, and M. P. Loeb: "Evaluating Information Security Investments Using the Analytic Hierarchy Process." *Communications of the ACM*, vol. 48. no. 2, February 2005, pp. 78–83.

Brealey, R. A., and S. C. Myers: *Principles of Corporate Finance*, 6th ed. New York: McGraw-Hill, 2000.

Bush, G. W.: "Executive Order 13231 on Critical Infrastructure Protection." Oct. 16, 2001. Available at http://www.white-house.gov/news/releases/2001/10/20011016-12.html.

California Security Breach Information Act (S.B. 1386), February 2002. Available at http://info.sen.ca.gov/pub/01-02/bill/sen/sb_1351-1400/sb_1386_bill_20020926_chaptered.html.

Camp, L. J., and C. Wolfram: "Pricing Security." *Proceedings of the CERT Information Survivability Workshop,* October 2000.

Campbell, K., L. A. Gordon, M. P. Loeb, and L. Zhou: "The Economic Cost of Publicly Announced Information Security Breaches: Empirical Evidence from the Stock Market." *Journal of Computer Security,* vol. 11, no. 3, 2003, pp. 431–448.

Cavusoglu, H., B. Mishra, and S. Raghunathan: "A Model for Evaluating IT Security Investments." *Communications of the ACM,* vol. 47, no. 7, July 2004, pp. 87–92.

CERT Coordination Center. *CERT/CC Statistics* 1988–2004. Available at http://www.cert.org/2004/.

Clinger-Cohen Act of 1996. Formerly known as the Information Technology Management Reform Act. Available at http://gov-info.library.unt.edu/npr/library/misc/s1124.html.

Commission on the Intelligence Capabilities of the United States Regarding Weapons of Mass Destruction, Mar. 31, 2005. Available at http://www.wmd.gov/report/wmd_report.pdf.

Committee of Sponsoring Organizations of the Treadway Commission: "Enterprise Risk Management—Integrated Framework: Executive Summary." September 2004. Available at http://www.coso.org/publications.htm.

Computer Security Act of 1987 (Public Law 100-235). Available at http://www.osec.doc.gov/cio/oipr/ITSec/csa-1987.html.

Computer Security Industry Alliance Newsletter, vol. 1, no. 3, November 2004. Available at https://www.csialliance.org/news/newsletters/newsletter_nov-04.html.

Corporate Information Security Accountability Act of 2003 (draft). Available at http://www.unsecureprivacy.com/CorpSecurPutnam.pdf.

Cyber Security Industry Alliance, "Sarbanes-Oxley Act: Implementation of Information Technology and Security Objectives." December 2004. Available at https://www.csialliance.org/resources/pdfs/CSIA_SOX_Report.pdf

Dean, J.: *Managerial Economics*. Englewood Cliffs, N.J.: Prentice-Hall, 1951.

Department of Defense Standard: Department of Defense Trusted Computer System Evaluation Criteria (aka the Orange Book). DoD 5200.28-STD, December 1985. Available at http://www.dynamoo.com/orange/fulltext.htm.

Dixit, A. K., and R. S. Pindyck: *Investment under Uncertainty*. Princeton, N.J.: Princeton University Press, 1994.

Federal Information Security Management Act (FISMA) of 2002. Available at http://csrc.nist.gov/policies/FISMA-final.pdf.

Gansler, J. S., and W. Lucyshyn: "Improving the Security of Financial Management Systems: What Are We to Do?" *Journal of Accounting and Public Policy*, vol. 24, no. 1, 2005, pp. 1–9.

Gates, B., and S. A. Ballmer: "Shareholder Letter," Microsoft Corporation 2004 Annual Report, Sept. 1, 2004.

General Accounting Office (GAO): "Critical Infrastructure Protection: Comprehensive Strategy Can Draw on Year 2000 Experiences." GAO/AIMD-00-1, October 1999.

General Accounting Office (GAO): "Executive Guide: Information Security Management: Learning from Leading Organizations." GAO/AIMD-98-68, May 1998.

Gordon, L. A.: *Managerial Accounting: Concepts and Empirical Evidence*, 6th ed. New York: McGraw-Hill, 2004.

Gordon, L. A., and M. P. Loeb: "A Framework for Using Information Security as a Response to Competitor Analysis Systems." *Communications of the ACM*, vol. 44, no. 9, September 2001a, pp.70–75.

Gordon, L. A., and M. P. Loeb: "Economic Aspects of Information Security." *Tech Trends Notes,* Fall 2001b.

Gordon, L. A., and M. P. Loeb: "The Economics of Information Security Investment." *ACM Transactions on Information and System Security*, vol. 5, no. 4, November 2002a, pp. 438–457.

Gordon, L. A., and M. P. Loeb: "Return on Information Security Investments: Myths vs. Reality." *Strategic Finance*, November 2002b, pp. 26–31.

Gordon, L. A., and M. P. Loeb: "Expenditures on Competitor Analysis and Information Security: A Management Accounting Perspective," chapter 5 in A. Bhimini (ed.), *Management Accounting in the Digital Economy*. Oxford, U.K.: Oxford University Press, 2003.

Gordon, L. A., and M. P. Loeb: "Budgeting Process for Information Security Expenditures: Empirical Evidence," forthcoming in *Communications of the ACM*.

Gordon, L. A., M. P. Loeb, and W. Lucyshyn: "Information Security Expenditures and Real Options: A Wait and See Approach." *Computer Security Journal,* vol. 19, no. 2, Spring 2003a, pp.1–7.

Gordon, L. A., M. P. Loeb, and W. Lucyshyn: "Sharing Information on Computer Systems Security: An Economic Analysis." *Journal of Accounting and Public Policy*, vol. 22, no. 6, 2003b, pp. 461–485.

Gordon, L. A., M. P. Loeb, W. Lucyshyn, and R. Richardson: "2004 CSI/FBI Computer Crime and Security Survey." *Computer Security Journal*, vol. 20, no. 3, Summer 2004, pp. 33–51.

Gordon, L. A., M. P. Loeb, and T. Sohail: "A Framework for Using Insurance for Cyber Risk Management." *Communications of the ACM,* vol. 46, no. 3, March 2003, pp. 81–85.

Government Technology: "Federal CIO Council Creates Information Security Exchange." Feb. 22, 2005. Available at http://www.govtech.net/ magazine/channel_story.php?channel=17&id=93148.

Gramm-Leach-Bliley Act of 1999 (S. 900). Available at http://www.ftc.gov/privacy/glbact/glboutline.htm.

Health Insurance Portability and Accountability Act of 1996 (H.R. 3103). Available at http://aspe.hhs.gov/admnsimp/pl104191.htm.

Homeland Security Act of 2002 (H.R. 5005-3). Available at http://www.dhs.gov/interweb/assetlibrary/hr_5005_enr.pdf.

Hoo, K.: "How Much Is Enough? A Risk-Management Approach to Computer Security." *Consortium for Research on Information Security Policy (CRISP) Working Paper*. Stanford University, Stanford, Calif., June 2000.

Information Systems Security Association, "Generally Accepted Information Security Principles (GAISP), version 3.0," 2004. Available at http://www.issa.org/gaisp/_pdfs/v30.pdf.

International Chamber of Commerce (ICC). Available at http://www.icccwbo.org/index.asp.

International Organization for Standardization, ISO/IEC 177999: 2000, "Information Technology—Code of Practice for Information Security Management," 2004. Available at http://www.iso.ch/ iso/en/CatalogueDetailPage.CatalogueDetail?CSNUMBER=33441&ICS1= 35&ICS2=&ICS3.

Internet Society. "A Brief History of the Internet," 2003. Available at http://www.isoc.org/internet/history/brief.shtml.

Karygiannis, T., and L. Owens: "Wireless Network Security: 802.11, Bluetooth and Handheld Devices." Computer Security Division, Information Technology Laboratory, National Institute of Standards and Technology, November 2002.

Koch, C.: "The Sarbox Conspiracy." *CIO Magazine,* July 1, 2004.

Krishnan, R., M. Smith, and R. Telang: "The Economics of Peer to Peer Networks." *Journal of Information Technology Theory and Application*, vol. 5, no. 3, 2003, pp. 31–44.

Lajoux, A., and J. F. Weston: *The Art of M&A Financing: Sources and Instruments for Growth*. New York: McGraw-Hill, 1999.

Leyden, J.: "European Cyber Security Agency Is a Go." *The Register*, Nov. 21, 2003. Available at http://www.theregister.co.uk/2003/11/21/european_cyber_security_agency/print.html.

National Bureau of Standards: Federal Information Processing Standard (FIPS) 65. *Guideline for Automatic Data Process Risk Analysis*, 1975.

National Commission on Terrorist Attacks: *The 9/11 Commission Report: Final Report of the National Commission on Terrorist Attacks upon the United States*. New York: W. W. Norton, 2004.

National Intelligence Reform Act of 2004. Available at http://www.theorator.com/bills108/s2845.html.

National Institute of Standards and Technology (NIST): *An Intro-duction to Computer Security: The NIST Handbook.* Special Publication 800-12, 1995.

National Institute of Standards and Technology (NIST): *Federal Information Processing Standards.* Available at http://csrc.nist.gov/publications/fips/.

Odlyzko, A.: "Privacy, Economics, and Price Discrimination on the Internet." ACM, *Fifth International Conference on Electronic Commerce,* 2003.

Office of the Prime Minister of Canada: "Government of Canada Releases Comprehensive National Security Policy." Apr. 27, 2004. Available at http://pm.gc.ca/eng/news.asp?id=186.

Organization for Economic Co-operation and Development (OECD): "Guidelines for the Security of Information Systems and Networks." Available at http://www.oecd.org/dataoecd/16/22/15582260.pdf.

Pindyck, R. S.: "Irreversibility, Uncertainty and Investment." *Journal of Economic Literature,* vol. 29, no. 3, September 1991, pp. 1110–1148.

Ridge, T.: "Transcript of Secretary of Homeland Security Tom Ridge at Press Conference." Nov. 30, 2004. Available at http://news.yahoo.com/news?tmpl=story&u= /usnw/20041130/pl_usnw/transcript_of_secretary_of_homeland_security_tom_ridge_at_press_conference145_xml.

Saranow, J., and R. Lieber: "Freezing Out Identity Theft: Potent State Laws Let Consumers Bar Access to Credit Reports, but Not Without Headaches." *Wall Street Journal,* Mar. 15, 2005.

Sarbanes-Oxley Act of 2002 (PL 107-204, July 30, 2002). Available at http://news.findlaw.com/hdocs/docs/gwbush/sarbanesoxley072302.pdf.

Saxton, F.: Foreword to "Security in the Information Age," Joint Economic Committee, United States Congress, May 2002.

Scharfstein, D. S., and J. C. Stein: "Herd Behavior and Investment," *American Economic Review,* vol. 80, no. 3, 1990, pp. 465–479.

Schechter, S., and M. Smith: "How Much Security Is Enough to Stop a Thief? The Economics of Outsider Theft via Computer Systems and Networks," in *Proceedings of the Financial Cryptography Conference.* Gosier, Guadeloupe, Jan. 27–30, 2003.

Securities Act of 1933. Available at http://www.sec.gov/divisions/corpfin/33act/index1933.shtml.

Securities Exchange Act of 1934. Available at http://www.sec.gov/divisions/corpfin/34act/index1934.shtml.

Shapiro, C., and H. Varian: *Information Rules: A Strategic Guide to the Network Economy.* Boston, MA.: Harvard Business School Press, 1988.

Simon, H. A.: *Administrative Behavior,* 2d ed. New York: Free Press, 1957.

Stahl, S.: "Is Your Customer Data Really Safe?" *Information Week,* May 30, 2005, p. 6.

Stoneburner, G., C. Hayden, and A. Feringa: "Engineering Principles for Information Technology Security (A Baseline for Achieving Security)." National Institute for Standards and Technology Special Publication 800-27, 2001. Available at http://csrc.nist.gov/publications/nistpubs/800-27/sp800-27.pdf.

Subcommittee on Technology, Information Policy, Intergovernmental Relations and the Census: "2003 Federal Computer Security Report Card." Dec. 9, 2003. Available at http://www.

reform.house.gov/UploadedFiles/Computer%20Security%20 Report %20card%202%20years.pdf.

Subcommittee on Technology, Information Policy, Intergovernmental Relations and the Census: "2004 Federal Computer Security Report Card." Feb. 16, 2005. Available at http:// reform.house.gov/UploadedFiles/2004%20Computer%20Sec urity%20Report%20card%202%20years.pdf.

Swanson, M., and B. Guttman: "Generally Accepted Principles and Practices for Securing Information Technology." National Institute for Standards and Technology Special Publication 800-14, 1996. Available at http://csrc.nist.gov/publications/ nistpubs/800-14/800-14.pdf.

U.S. Department of Homeland Security: "Ridge Creates New Division to Combat Cyber Threats." Press release dated June 6, 2003. Available at http://www.dhs.gov/dhspublic/display? content=916.

U.S. Department of Homeland Security: "U.S. Department of Homeland Security Improves America's Cyber Security Preparedness—Unveils National Cyber Alert System." Press release dated Jan. 28, 2004. Available at http://www.dhs.gov/dhspublic/ display?content=3086.

U.S. Department of Justice: "White Paper, The Clinton Administration's Policy on Critical Infrastructure Protection: Presidential Decision Directive 63." May 22, 1998. Available at http://www.usdoj.gov/criminal/cybercrime/white_pr.htm.

U.S. Embassy in Tokyo, Japan: "U.S.-Japan Joint Statement on Cyber Security." Sept. 9, 2003. Available at http://japan.usembassy.gov/e/p/tp-20030909d2.html.

U.S. Office of Homeland Security: "National Strategy for Homeland Security." July 2002. Available at http://www.whitehouse.gov/homeland/book/nat_strat_hls.pdf.

U.S. Securities and Exchange Commission: "Comments on Proposed Rule: Shareholder Reports and Quarterly Portfolio Disclosure of Registered Management Investment Companies Final Rule: Management's Reports on Internal Control over Financial Reporting and Certification of Disclosure in Exchange Act Periodic Reports." Release Nos. 33-8238, 34-47986; IC-26068; File Nos.: S7-40-02; S7-06-03. Available at http://www.sec.gov/rules/final/33-8238.htm.

U.S. Securities and Exchange Commission: "Final Rule: Management's Reports on Internal Control over Financial Reporting and Certification of Disclosure in Exchange Act Periodic Reports." Release Nos. 33-8238, 34-47986; IC-26068; File Nos.: S7-40-02; S7-06-03; June 5, 2003. Available at http://www.sec.gov/rules/final/33-8238.htm.

White House: "White Paper: The Clinton Administration's Policy on Critical Infrastructure Protection: Presidential Decision Directive 63." May 22, 1988. Available at http://www.fas.org/irp/offdocs/paper598.htm.

White House: "The National Strategy for the Physical Protection of Critical Infrastructures and Key Assets." February 2003a. Available at http://www.whitehouse.gov/pcipb/physical_strategy.pdf.

White House: "The National Strategy to Secure Cyberspace." February 2003b. Available at http://www.whitehouse.gov/pcipb/cyberspace_strategy.pdf.

SELECTED
ANNOTATED
BIBLIOGRAPHY

Anderson, R.: "Why Information Security Is Hard—An Economic Perspective," *Proceedings of the 17th Annual Computer Security Applications Conference*, December 2001. This paper argues that many computer security problems arise largely because of perverse economic incentives. Reliance on mere technical solutions, such as strengthened cryptographic protocols or better access control, in the absence of a thorough understanding of the economic setting is not likely to be fruitful. The paper is one of the first to introduce a number of well-known economic concepts, such as information asymmetry, moral hazard, switching costs, network externalities, price differentiation, and the market for "lemons" in the context of security engineering.

Asquiti, A.: "Privacy and Security of Personal Information: Economic Incentives and Technological Solutions," chapter 14 in L. Camp and S. Lewis (eds.), *Economics of Information Security*. Springer, 2004. Economists have been concerned with the issue of privacy and its relationship to social welfare for some time. This paper traces the development of the economics of privacy, with particular emphasis on recent studies applying microeconomic analysis to issues of privacy in the context of computer networks and e-commerce. Some studies show that consumers' demand for privacy as revealed by their actions is a lot less than the demand indicated by their words. In this regard, the paper discusses the benefits to individuals of sharing private information as well as the costs. Moreover, while technologies are available to increase privacy in cyberspace, there are insufficient economic incentives for consumers or vendors to adopt the strongest technologies. The paper also examines the role of distinguishing between protecting an individual's on-line identity and off-line identity in analyzing issues of privacy.

Bagchi, K., and G. Udo: "An Analysis of the Growth of Computer and Internet Security Breaches," *Communications of the Association for Information Systems*, vol. 12, December 2003, pp. 680–700. Growth rates and patterns for different types of security breaches (e.g., Web defacement and denial-of-service attacks) are investigated in this paper using a diffusion model that was previously used to investigate collective violence in the sociology literature. The model takes into account that as attacks spread, preventive efforts to quell breaches are triggered. The data analyzed are taken from seven years of the CSI/FBI Computer Crime and Security Surveys. One conclusion of the paper is that since different cybercrimes are growing at different rates, the attention (and hence the resources) devoted to these crimes should also differ.

Bodin, L., L. A. Gordon, and M. P. Loeb: "Evaluating Information Security Investments Using the Analytic Hierarchy Process," *Communications of the ACM*, February 2005, pp. 78–83. The analytic hierarchy process (AHP) is a tool for analyzing multi-criteria decision problems involving quantitative and qualitative criteria. This paper shows how a chief information security officer can apply the AHP to determine the best way to spend a limited information security budget and to make a case to the organization's chief financial officer for an increase in funds to further enhance the organization's information security.

Camp, L. J., and C. Wolfram: "Pricing Security," *Proceedings of the CERT Information Survivability Workshop,* October 2000. This paper argues that an alternative solution to security vulnerabilities is to create a market for the detection of security failures. Using the analogy of pollution credits, the authors introduce the concept of tradable vulnerability credits in order to use the power of the market system to enhance software security. The authors claim that an adoption of this approach as economic policy will be beneficial for society.

Campbell, K., L. A. Gordon, M. P. Loeb, and L. Zhou: "The Economic Cost of Publicly Announced Information Security Breaches: Empirical Evidence from the Stock Market," *Journal of Computer Security*, vol. 11, no. 3, 2003, pp. 431–448. This study examines the economic effect of information security breaches on the stock market value of corporations. This approach takes into account the indirect costs, as well as the direct costs, to the firm. The analysis shows that cybersecurity breaches in which confidential private information is compromised (e.g., the release of customer credit card numbers, bank account numbers, or medical records to unauthorized parties) have a significant negative effect on the stock market value of the attacked firm. However, security breaches that are not related to confidentiality (e.g., a temporary shutdown of a corporate Web site) involve costs that are transitory and are unlikely to significantly affect shareholder value. Thus, market participants appear to discriminate across types of breaches, and economically rational investment strategies should focus on protecting the firms' most valuable information assets.

Cavusoglu, H., B. Mishra, and S. Raghunathan: "A Model for Evaluating IT Security Investments," *Communications of the ACM*, vol. 47, no. 7, July 2004, pp. 87–92. This paper presents an analytical model in an attempt to facilitate decisions regarding security investments. The model presented incorporates specific features of the technologies used in a typical IT security infrastructure. An important feature of the model described in the paper is that it provides insight into evaluating the interaction among different technologies and deciding on investments in multiple technologies.

Clinger-Cohen Act of 1996. Available at http://govinfo.library. unt.edu/npr/library/misc/s1124.html. This act, formerly known as the Information Technology Management Reform Act, streamlines information technology acquisitions and emphasizes life-cycle management of IT as a capital investment. Among the key actions are the return of IT procurement authority to agencies; the elimination of the Federal Information Resources Management Regulation (FIRMR); the integration of the IT management process with the processes for making budget, financial, and program management decisions; and the establishment of goals for improving the efficiency and effectiveness of agency operations.

Commission on the Intelligence Capabilities of the United States Regarding Weapons of Mass Destruction, Mar. 31, 2005. Available at http://www.wmd.gov/report/wmd_report.pdf. This report evaluates the performance of the United States' intelligence community "in assessing the nuclear, biological, and chemical weapons activities of three countries: Iraq, Afghanistan, and Libya." In addition, the commission examined the U.S. capabilities against "other pressing intelligence problems—including Iran, North Korea, Russia, China, and terrorism." In the final analysis, this report documents "one of the most public—and damaging—intelligence failures in recent American history." After documenting the intelligence failures, the report goes on to make numerous specific recommendations for improving the situation. However, as noted in the commission's report, "perhaps the single most prominent and recurring theme in our recommendations is a call for stronger and more centralized management of the intelligence community, and, in general, the creation of a genuinely integrated community instead of a loose confederation of independent agencies. This is not a new idea, but it has never been successfully implemented."

Computer Security Act of 1987 (Public Law 100-235, approved Jan. 8, 1988, 101 Stat. 1724-1730). Available at http://www.osec.doc. gov/cio/oipr/ITSec/csa-1987.html. This piece of legislation is intended to generally improve the security and privacy of "sensitive information" in federal computer systems. The specific objectives of the act are "to assign to the National Bureau of Standards [now the National Institute of Standards and Technology] responsibility for developing standards and guidelines for Federal computer systems, including responsibility for developing standards and guidelines needed to assure the cost-effective security and privacy of sensitive information in Federal computer systems, drawing on the technical advice and assistance (including work products) of the National Security Agency, where appropriate; to provide for promulgation of such standards and guidelines by amending section 111(d) of the Federal Property and Administrative Services Act of 1949; to require establishment of security plans by all operators of Federal computer systems that contain sensitive information; and to require mandatory periodic training for all persons involved in management, use, or operation of Federal computer systems that contain sensitive information."

Department of Defense Standard: Department of Defense Trusted Computer System Evaluation Criteria (aka the Orange Book). DoD 5200.28-STD, December 1985. Available at http://www. dynamoo.com/orange/fulltext.htm. This document provides trusted computer system evaluation criteria. The objectives of these criteria are "(1) To provide a standard to manufacturers as to what security features to build into their new and planned, commercial products in order to provide widely available systems that satisfy trust requirements (with particular emphasis on preventing the disclosure of data) for sensitive applications. (2) To provide DoD components with a metric that can evaluate the degree of trust that can be placed in computer systems for the secure processing of classified and other sensitive information. (3) To provide a basis for specifying security requirements in acquisition specifications." The six fundamental computer security requirements specified in this document became known as "the Orange Book" and were considered the minimum standards for vendors to follow when selling computer systems to DoD. The Orange Book was originally published in 1983 (the reference given here is an update of the original 1983 document). According to many, the Orange Book is still the key standard for computer security today.

Federal Information Security Management Act (FISMA) of 2002. Available at http://csrc.nist.gov/policies/FISMA-final.pdf. This law is contained within the E-Government Act of 2002 (Public Law 107-347), replacing the Government Information Security

Reform Act (GISRA). FISMA, effective throughout the federal government, places requirements on government agencies and components with the goal of improving the security of federal information and information systems. FISMA requires U.S. federal government agencies with an inspector general to conduct annual reviews of their information security program. The results of these reviews need to be reported to the Office of Management and Budget (OMB), which in turn prepares a report to Congress on the status of the information security of the different agencies. FISMA also requires that the agencies report the results of their information security reviews to Congress and the Government Accountability Office. As a result of the information contained in these reports, Congress's Government Reform Committee prepares a FISMA Report Card that grades the various agencies on computer security.

Gansler, J. S., and W. Lucyshyn: "Improving the Security of Financial Management Systems: What are we to do?," *Journal of Accounting and Public Policy*, vol. 24, no. 1, 2005, pp. 1–9. After discussing the impact of cybersecurity to financial management systems, this paper describes impediments to providing adequate cybersecurity and realistic strategies to enhance cybersecurity. The impediments examined are (1) the dynamic nature of the problem, i.e., threats and vulnerabilities are constantly changing, (2) attacks are able to launched by adversaries with little technical expertise, (3) difficulty in estimating the risk associated with attacks, and (4) enhancing cybersecurity is hard. The paper discusses the following strategies for enhancing cybersecurity: (1) ensuring that the enterprise has a high-ranking manager acting as a champion for improving cybersecurity, (2) developing a systems approach to security, (3) improving software, and (4) improving information sharing.

Gordon, L. A., and M. P. Loeb: "Economic Aspects of Information Security," *Tech Trends Notes,* Fall 2001. This paper provides an economic framework for looking at the allocation of resources to information security activities. A major argument of this paper is that expenditures on information security need to be considered in cost-benefit terms in a fashion similar to the way organizations allocate resources to other activities.

Gordon, L. A., and M. P. Loeb: "A Framework for Using Information Security as a Response to Competitor Analysis Systems," *Communications of the ACM,* vol. 44, no. 9, September 2001, pp.70–75. Information security is an appropriate response to rivals' development of competitor analysis systems. This paper provides a framework for using information security in such a way. The paper also provides a five-step approach to allocating information security funds in an effort to protect a firm from becoming a meaningful part of the competition's competitor analysis system.

Gordon, L. A., and M. P. Loeb: "The Economics of Information Security Investment," *ACM Transactions on Information and System Security,* vol. 5, no. 4, November 2002, pp. 438–457. This paper presents an economic model that characterizes the optimal monetary investment to protect a given set of information. It is shown that, for a given potential loss, the optimal amount to spend to protect an information set does not always increase with increases in the information set's vulnerability. Protecting highly vulnerable information sets may be inordinately expensive, and a firm may be better off concentrating its efforts on information sets with mid-range vulnerabilities. Moreover, the paper shows that the amount the firm should spend to protect information sets should generally be only a small fraction of the expected loss.

Gordon, L. A., and M. P. Loeb: "Return on Information Security Investments: Myths vs. Reality," *Strategic Finance*, November 2002, pp. 26–31. Although measures of return on investment have gained increased attention as a financial tool for evaluating information security projects, conceptual and practical problems with these measures have been largely ignored. This paper highlights several of these problems. The paper shows that the common accounting measure of return on investment is different from the economic measure of return on investment, and that the accounting measure is inappropriate for both the ex ante and ex post evaluation of information security projects. The paper also recommends focusing on selecting a profit-maximizing level of information security investment as opposed to the investment level that maximizes a measure of return on investment.

Gordon, L. A., and M. P. Loeb: "Expenditures on Competitor Analysis and Information Security: A Management Accounting Perspective," chapter 5 in A. Bhimini (ed.), *Management Accounting in the Digital Economy*. Oxford, U.K.: Oxford University Press, 2003. An underlying premise for both expenditures on competitor analysis and expenditures on information security is that information is an economic good with strategic value. In this paper, a game theoretic model of a market shared by two rivals is presented and analyzed in order to shed light on how expenditures on competitor analysis affect, and are affected by, expenditures on information security. The paper also discusses the importance of these information economy–based issues for management accounting.

Gordon, L A., M. P. Loeb, and W. Lucyshyn: "Information Security Expenditures and Real Options: A Wait-and-See Approach," *Computer Security Journal*, vol. 19, no. 2, 2003, pp. 1–7. Empirical evidence suggests that security breaches are an important driver of actual expenditures on information security activities. Although this wait-and-see approach toward information security expenditures may seem unwise on the surface, there is a rational economic explanation for such an approach under the appropriate conditions. Indeed, as shown in this paper, this approach to information security expenditures may be consistent with the real option (in particular, the deferment option) view of capital budgeting.

Gordon, L. A., M. P. Loeb, and W. Lucyshyn: "Sharing Information on Computer Systems Security: An Economic Analysis," *Journal of Accounting and Public Policy*, vol. 22, no. 6, 2003, pp. 461–485. The U.S. federal government has fostered a movement toward sharing information concerning computer security, with particular emphasis on protecting critical infrastructure assets that are largely owned by the private sector. This paper presents a model for examining the welfare economic implications of this movement. It is shown that, since information sharing lowers the cost of each firm's attaining any given level of information security, there are potential benefits for individual firms and society at large from sharing. However, it is also shown that in the absence of appropriate economic incentive mechanisms, each firm will attempt to free-ride on the security expenditures of other firms (i.e., renege on the sharing agreement and refuse to share information).

Gordon, L. A., M. P. Loeb, W. Lucyshyn, and R. Richardson: "2004 CSI/FBI Computer Crime and Security Survey," *Computer Security Journal*, Summer 2004, pp. 33–51. This paper provides a summary of the findings from the ninth annual survey conducted by the CSI and the FBI on issues related to computer security. A key finding from the 2004 survey is the fact that a large percentage of organizations are starting to use economic metrics, such as ROI (return on investment), NPV (net present value), and IRR (internal rate of return), in allocating and evaluating computer security expenditures. Other key findings from the 2004 survey reported in this paper are (1) unauthorized use of computer systems, as well as the reporting of computer intrusions to law enforcement, is on the decline, (2) the Sarbanes-Oxley Act of 2002 is starting to have an important impact on computer security activities, (3) information security audits are being used by over 80 percent of the organizations responding to the survey, (4) most organizations do not outsource their computer security activities, and among those that do some outsourcing, the portion of security activities outsourced is quite low, and (5) organizations recognize the need to improve their security awareness training.

Gordon, L. A., M. P. Loeb, and T. Sohail: "A Framework for Using Insurance for Cyber Risk Management," *Communications of the ACM*, vol. 46, no. 3, March 2003, pp. 81–85. Insurance companies, in designing new policies to deal with the cyber risks of information breaches, have had to address issues related to pricing, adverse selection, and moral hazard. While these issues are common to all forms of insurance, this paper examines the unique aspects associated with cyber risk and presents a framework for using insurance as a tool for helping to manage information security risk. This framework is based on the risk management process and includes a four-step cyber risk insurance decision plan.

Gramm-Leach-Bliley Act of 1999 (S. 900): Available at http://www. ftc.gov/privacy/glbact/glboutline.htm. This act outlines privacy provisions relating to consumers' financial information. Financial institutions have restrictions on when they may disclose a consumer's personal financial information to nonaffiliated third parties. In addition, financial institutions are required to provide notices to their customers about their information-collection and information-sharing practices and allow customers to opt out if they do not want their information shared with third parties.

Health Insurance Portability and Accountability Act of 1996 (H.R. 3103): Available at http://aspe.hhs.gov/admnsimp/pl104191. htm. This act improves the portability and continuity of health insurance coverage in the group and individual markets and addresses issues related to protecting the confidentiality of clients' medical records. It also combats waste, fraud, and abuse in health insurance and health-care delivery; promotes the use of medical savings accounts; improves access to long-term care services and coverage; and simplifies the administration of health insurance.

Homeland Security Act of 2002 (H.R. 5005-3): Available at http://www.dhs.gov/interweb/assetlibrary/hr_5005_enr.pdf. This act established the Department of Homeland Security as an executive department within the United States. The primary mission of the Department is to (1) prevent terrorist attacks within the United States, (2) reduce the vulnerability of the United States to terrorism, and (3) minimize the damage and assist in the recovery from terrorist attacks that do occur within the United States.

Krishnan, R., M. Smith, and R. Telang: "The Economics of Peer to Peer Networks," *Journal of Information Technology Theory and Application*, vol. 5, no. 3, 2003, pp. 31–44. This article provides an interesting discussion about the sharing of resources among users of peer-to-peer (P2P) networks. In particular, it addresses important economic issues related to P2P networks. For example, such economic issues as public and club goods, the role of economic incentives, and reputation mechanisms are discussed in order to shed new light on the efficient operation of P2P networks.

National Commission on Terrorist Attacks: *The 9/11 Commission Report: Final Report of the National Commission on Terrorist Attacks upon the United States.* New York: W. W. Norton, 2004. This book includes the findings and recommendations of an independent, bipartisan panel that was established in November 2002 by the U.S. Congress and President George W. Bush and given the task of examining the facts and circumstances surrounding the September 11 attacks. The book identifies lessons learned and provides recommendations to safeguard against future acts of terrorism.

National Institute of Standards and Technology (NIST): *An Introduction to Computer Security: The NIST Handbook.* Special Publication 800-12, 1995. This handbook provides a "broad overview of computer security to help readers understand their computer security needs and develop a sound approach to the selection of appropriate security controls." The breadth, depth, and clarity of this handbook are excellent and have made this document one of the most highly referenced in the computer security field. The range of issues covered in this handbook include threats to computer security, computer security policy and risk management, personnel concerns, handling incidents, training and education, physical security, logical access control, auditing, and cryptography.

National Intelligence Reform Act of 2004: Available at http://www.theorator.com/bills108/s2845.html. This law seeks to reform the intelligence community and the intelligence and intelligence-related activities of the U.S. government by establishing the National Intelligence Authority as an independent agency within the executive branch of the U.S. government. This independent agency is headed by the national intelligence director. The National Intelligence Reform Act also includes recommendations from the 9/11 Commission Report and modifications to existing laws related to intelligence community management.

Odlyzko, A.: "Privacy, Economics, and Price Discrimination on the Internet." ACM, *Fifth International Conference on Electronic Commerce*, 2003. The loss of privacy, a cybersecurity issue, is examined and explained in this paper. The Internet provides organizations with the opportunity to collect information more easily about individual consumers' willingness to pay for goods or services. This facilitates a firm's ability to increase its income by charging different prices to different consumers (i.e., price discrimination). While price discrimination leads to efficient allocation of resources, many individual consumers (those with a high willingness to pay) are worse off than when firms charge a uniform price. Since firms have the incentive to collect private information, a continued loss of privacy and use of variants of price discrimination are predicted.

Organization for Economic Co-operation and Development (OECD): "Guidelines for the Security of Information Systems and Networks: Towards a Culture of Security." Available at http://www.oecd.org/dataoecd/16/22/15582260.pdf. These guidelines give particular attention to the interconnectivity of information systems and networks brought about by the Internet. The guidelines consist of the following set of nine complementary principles that participants using the systems and networks need to consider: (1) *awareness* of the need for security, (2) *responsibility* for security, (3) timely and cooperative *response* to security issues, (4) respect for the rights of others, (5) compatibility with the values of a *democratic* society, (6) *risk assessment* of threats and vulnerabilities, (7) proper *security design and implementation*, (8) a comprehensive approach to *security management*, and (9) periodic *reassessment* of security policies, practices, measures, and procedures. These guidelines were adopted on July 25, 2002, and replaced OECD's 1992 "Guidelines for the Security of Information Systems."

Sarbanes-Oxley Act of 2002 (PL 107-204, July 30, 2002): Available at http://news.findlaw.com/hdocs/docs/gwbush/sarbanes-oxley072302.pdf. This act was designed to protect investors by improving the accuracy and reliability of corporate disclosures made pursuant to the securities laws and for other purposes. This act addresses issues including the establishment of a public company accounting oversight board, auditor independence, corporate responsibility, enhanced financial disclosures, analyst conflicts of interest, and corporate and criminal fraud accountability, among others. In terms of financial disclosure and corporate governance, this act is probably the most important piece of legislation in the United States since the Securities Act of 1933 and the Securities Exchange Act of 1934.

Schechter, S., and M. Smith: "How Much Security Is Enough to Stop a Thief: The Economics of Outsider Theft via Computer Systems and Networks," in *Proceedings of the* Financial Cryptography Conference, Gosier, Guadeloupe, Jan. 27–30, 2003. This paper models the expected profits to a thief of exploiting a single vulnerability in a packaged system that has been installed in multiple organizations. The probability that a given organization's system will be attacked depends on the potential benefits that the thief can derive from attacking all the user organizations, as well as the preventive actions taken by all the user organizations. Thus, users of a packaged system have a shared economic interest in thwarting attacks. The model implies that organizations may find sharing of information about intrusion detection and response strategies to be a cost-effective strategy in deterring cyber attacks.

Shapiro, C. L., and H. R. Varian: *Information Rules: A Strategic Guide to the Network Economy.* Cambridge, MA.: Harvard Business School Press, 1988. This book presents fundamental economic principles as applied to the Internet and the production and sale of information goods. The concepts of information goods, network effects, standardization, switching costs, lock-in, digital rights, market segmentation, versioning, and pricing are discussed, using numerous examples ranging from traditional books to HDTV and software. The authors go beyond explaining numerous economic concepts and indicate how a businessperson can use these concepts to develop strategies to enhance profitability.

White House: "White Paper: The Clinton Administration's Policy on Critical Infrastructure Protection: Presidential Decision Directive 63," May 22, 1988. Available at http://www.fas.org/irp/offdocs/paper598.htm. This presidential directive builds on the recommendations of the President's Commission on Critical Infrastructure Protection. The president's policy sets a goal of a reliable, interconnected, and secure information system infrastructure by the year 2003; addresses the cyber and physical infrastructure vulnerabilities of the federal government by requiring each department and agency to work to reduce its exposure to new threats; requires the federal government to serve as a model to the rest of the country for how infrastructure protection is to be attained; seeks the voluntary participation of private industry to meet common goals for protecting our critical systems through public-private partnerships; protects privacy rights; and seeks to utilize market forces.

White House: "The National Strategy to Secure Cyberspace,"
February 2003. Available at http://www.whitehouse.gov/
pcipb/ cyberspace_strategy.pdf. This document is part of an
overall effort to protect the United States by engaging and
empowering Americans to "secure the portions of cyberspace
that they own, operate, control or with which they interact." In
essence, this document provides a blueprint for securing the
U.S. cyberspace.

Index

ABOUT THE AUTHORS

Lawrence A. Gordon, Ph. D., is the Ernst & Young Alumni Professor of Managerial Accounting and Information Assurance and the director of the Ph.D. program at the Robert H. Smith School of Business. He is also an affiliate professor in the University of Maryland Institute for Advanced Computer Studies. Dr. Gordon earned his Ph.D. in Managerial Economics from Rensselaer Polytechnic Institute. An internationally known scholar in the area of managerial accounting and information security, Dr. Gordon's current research focuses on the economic aspects of information security, corporate performance measures, capital investments, and cost management systems. He is the author of more than 85 articles, published in such journals as *ACM Transactions on Information and System Security, Journal of Computer Security, The Accounting Review, Journal of Financial and Quantitative Analysis, Accounting Organizations and Society, Journal of Accounting and Public Policy, Decision Sciences, Omega, Journal of Business Finance and Accounting, Accounting and Business Research, Managerial and Decision Economics, Communications of the ACM,* and *Management Accounting Research.* Dr. Gordon also is the author of several books, including *Managerial Accounting: Concepts and Empirical Evidence* and *Capital Budgeting: A Decision Support System Approach.* In addition, he is the editor-in-chief of the *Journal of Accounting and Public Policy* and serves on the editorial boards of several other journals. In two recent studies, Dr. Gordon was cited as being among the world's most influential/productive accounting researchers. Dr. Gordon is also one of the pioneers in conducting research in the area of cybersecurity economics.

An award-winning teacher, Dr. Gordon has been an invited speaker at numerous universities around the world, including Harvard University, Columbia University, University of Toronto, London Business School, and London School of Economics. He also has served as a consultant to several private (e.g., IBM) and public (e.g., U.S. Government Accountability Office) organizations. Dr. Gordon's former Ph.D. students are currently distinguished faculty members at such universities as Stanford University, Ohio State University, Michigan State University, McGill University, The College of William and Mary, University of Southern California, and National Taiwan University. His former M.B.A. students frequently call him on the "Management Accounting Hotline" (as affectionately named by his students) to discuss issues confronting their organizations. Dr. Gordon also is a frequent contributor to the popular press (e.g., *Wall Street Journal, BusinessWeek, USA Today,* and *Financial Times*). For more information about Dr. Gordon, go to his Web site at the University of Maryland (http://www.rhsmith.umd.edu/faculty/lgordon/).

Martin P. Loeb, Ph. D., is a professor of Accounting and Information Assurance and a Deloitte & Touche Faculty Fellow at the Robert H. Smith School of Business, University of Maryland, College Park. He is also an affiliate professor in the University of Maryland Institute for Advanced Computer Studies. Dr. Loeb earned his Ph.D. in Managerial Economics and Decision Sciences from the Kellogg School of Management, Northwestern University. Before embarking on research concerning the economic aspects of information security, Professor Loeb was an early leader in research on mechanism design and incentive regulation that has had a broad impact on the fields of economics, computer science, accounting, and political science. His research on cost allocations and budget-based procurement contracting has also been influential.

Dr. Loeb's research papers have appeared in a variety of leading academic journals, including *ACM Transactions on Information and System Security, The Accounting Review, American Economic Review, Contemporary Accounting Research, Journal of Accounting Research, Journal of Banking and Finance, Journal of Computer Security, Journal of Law and Economics, Journal of Public Economics, Management Accounting Research, Managerial and Decision Economics,* and *Management Science.* Professor Loeb is an editor of the *Journal of Accounting and Public Policy* and serves or has served on the editorial boards of *The Accounting Review, British Accounting Review, Journal of Business Finance and Accounting,* and *Review of Accounting Studies.* For more information about Dr. Loeb, go to his Web site at the University of Maryland (http://www.rhsmith.umd.edu/faculty/mloeb/). Dr. Loeb is also one of the pioneers in conducting research in the area of cybersecurity economics.